DESIGNING YOUR OWN LANDSCAPE

DESIGNING YOUR OWN LANDSCAPE

*Plants and ways
to use them in the garden*

GORDON HAYWARD

ILLUSTRATIONS BY GORDON MORRISON

WHETSTONE PUBLISHING
Brattleboro, Vt 05301

A version of chapter 14 first appeared in *Fine Gardening*,
Box 355, Newtown, CT 06470.

Chapter 32 is reprinted from the April 1984 issue of *American
Horticulturist*, Box 0105, Mount Vernon, VA 22121.

Chapters 18–20 are reprinted with the courtesy of
Harrowsmith magazine, The Creamery, Charlotte, VT 05445.

Altered versions of chapters 2, 3, 5–13, 15–17, and 21–31
originally appeared in *Horticulture*, the Magazine of
American Gardening, The Statler Office Building, 20 Park Plaza,
Suite 1220, Boston, MA 02116. First serial rights to chapters 1
and 4 belong to *Horticulture*, and the chart in chapter 16
is used with that magazine's permission. Several of Gordon
Morrison's illustrations also first appeared in
Horticulture.

ISBN 0-9621439-1-X
Library of Congress card number 89-52065

Text design by Irving Perkins Associates
Cover design by James Brisson

Published by Whetstone Publishing
67 Main Street, Suite 42
Brattleboro, VT 05301

Manufactured in the United States of America

TO HOWARD

CONTENTS

TOOLS and TECHNIQUES 129

VEGETABLES 171

ACKNOWLEDGMENTS

First, thanks to Dennis Meacham, who, in 1977, was an editor at *Country Journal*, and who first encouraged me to write for publication; to Barbara George, who, in 1989, suggested that we create this book together; to Gordon Morrison for his fine illustrations; to Tom Cooper, Teri Blau, and especially John Barstow at *Horticulture Magazine*; to Nancy Olson, teacher, friend, and fellow writer.

Second, thanks to all the people who shared their knowledge and plants over the years: to Shepherd Ogden, Marion Andros, and Dymock Maurice; to Kristian Fenderson, Fred Watson, and Alice Holway; to Rosemary Verey, Ethne Clarke, and Christopher Lloyd; to George Cooper and the late John Broad, gardeners at the Hidcote Manor Gardens; to Mrs. Phyllis Jones, who has the best cottage garden in Gloucestershire; to Ian and Raz Maitland-Hume at Broadwell Manor, who really did get me started. Thanks also to my clients, who over the years trusted my eye.

Next, thanks to Bill Duffey and to my excellent crew who have helped me bring my ideas to fruition. Thanks to Peter and Theodora Berg, with whom I have shared countless happy hours on both sides of the Atlantic in the name of fine gardening. Thanks to Margaret Hensel for sharing her keen eye for design and her good sense about garden writing; I couldn't have written the first chapter without her. Thanks to Paul Smyth, who is both a good friend and a good writer. Heartfelt thanks to Howard Andros, a gentleman and mentor who has given unstintingly of his knowledge and sage advice. Thanks also to my parents—to my father, who, as I was growing up in our orchard in Connecticut, taught me how to care for our trees, the woods, and the natural world. And finally, thanks to my wife Mary and our son Nate for everything under the sun and moon.

INTRODUCTION

Gardening, often thought to be a solitary activity, in fact weaves a wide and complex web of associations with other gardeners. Over the years, as I've grown as a self-taught gardener and designer, I've been faced time and again with questions I couldn't answer on my own. To get answers to those questions, I talked with experts. In many ways this book is a record of my conversations with those people, from well-known authorities such as Christopher Lloyd and Penelope Hobhouse of England to New England friends and fellow gardeners such as Kristian Fenderson in Acworth, New Hampshire, or Howard Andros in Walpole, New Hampshire.

Twelve years ago, when my wife and I were living in her family's village just across the fields from the renowned Hidcote Manor Gardens in Gloucestershire, England, I took every opportunity to talk with John Broad and George Cooper, gardeners who worked there. Wherever we lived and gardened— in Stow-on-the-Wold in Gloucestershire where I restored a manor house garden, in Cornwall, Connecticut, in Alstead, New Hampshire, and now at our home in Westminster West, Vermont—I sought out those who knew a great deal about one facet or another of gardening.

As you read this book, a compilation of articles I wrote for *Horticulture, American Horticulturist, Harrowsmith*, and *Fine Gardening* magazines over the past 11 years, you'll find that other gardeners are mentioned in every chapter. Therein lies the theme, the thread that runs through this book. You feel a growing companionship as you garden. You learn to talk with others, whether expert or not, for everyone who has ever gardened thoughtfully has learned something worth sharing.

You then work with that knowledge, make it your own, and pass it on to others. I absorbed what Howard Andros taught me about perennials, and developed that knowledge to expand the variety of plants in my designs and to make more subtle color combinations with them. George Cooper taught me how to make a good dropped edge to a grass path. I took that technique and made it part of how I design perennial beds, so that paths link them and thus hold them in relationship to one another. Harold Epstein from Larchmont, New York, an expert on Japanese garden plants, taught me how he uses the climbing hydrangea in his garden. One now grows in our garden, in a way that makes sense in rural Vermont.

It's easy to feel awed and stymied by almost any facet of gardening or design. Yet confidence in ourselves, which grows with knowledge, is all we lack. The complex world of roses, for example, can be daunting, but it need not be. I knew enough about roses to grow them in our own garden, but before suggesting them for my clients I felt I had to learn more. So I visited Mike Lowe in Nashua, New Hampshire, one of the nation's top experts on the subject. I spent several days in his rose gardens with him, and also talked with him in the dead of winter, when rose cones covered his collection. The article I wrote was based on those conversations, but I also planted many roses I purchased from Mike so I could put into practice what he taught me.

Rich associations develop between the people and the plant, technique, or element of design we learn about from them. Jean and Hellen Gazagnaire, friends from West Cornwall, Connecticut, remembered buying salsify in Paris as children shopping with their mothers. We now grow salsify, and when we have it for dinner we think of the Gazagnaires. Howard Andros has gardened since he was a boy, tagging along behind E. H. Wilson, the eminent curator of the Arnold Arboretum in Boston, on Wilson's Sunday arboretum tours. Howard has given us many Saunders hybrid peonies—in fact, all the Saunders hybrids we have in our garden came from Howard, and so do all my associations with peonies. Margaret Hensel, a friend, fellow-gardener, and writer for *Horticulture* too, taught me a great deal about design, elements of which I associate with her.

As you read this book, I hope you'll find it suggests a way of thinking about plants and their history, about people and their gardens. That is, that gardening and gardeners are approachable. Everyone learns by doing. Penelope Hobhouse, the famous garden designer and writer, was educated as an economist. Howard Andros was a cartographer. I taught writing for 17 years. Harold Epstein was a New York businessman. Certainly there are many great gardeners and garden designers who had a formal horticultural education. But most are like you and me – people with a passion for the natural world, for color and design, and for healthy flourishing plants in their own gardens. They are people who are willing to take risks, to make mistakes, to experiment, and to learn.

Look long and hard and sensitively at the lay of the land around your house. Consider how you'll use your garden and live with it and in it. Chapter 1 outlines the steps you need to follow so you can make your own garden your own way, and gain confidence in your own abilities in the process. As you read on, remember that in the end the best garden is the one that best satisfies the gardener.

DESIGN

After years of designing my own garden and those of my clients, I wrote the first chapter of this collection for people like you who want to create your own landscape. It tells how I designed a particular garden in Vermont, but, more importantly, it explains universal design principles in a useful sequence. Read it and you should have the confidence to start work on your own garden design.

To develop the idea of residential garden design further, I include three more chapters. The first looks closely at plantings next to the house. The next considers space further out from the house in terms of how it will look in winter as well as during the growing season. The last chapter in this section tells how to develop a woodland walk so you can enjoy the pleasures inherent in the natural areas beyond the lawn.

1

DESIGNING YOUR OWN LANDSCAPE

Designing your own landscape need not be the overwhelming task we often consider it to be. If you organize the problems that have to be solved in a logical sequence, and then develop solutions to those problems, you can create a coherent and stimulating outdoor space for yourself, your family, and friends.

The sequence of decisions and the principles of design I followed in developing a plan for a small backyard garden in southern Vermont may help you give form to your own thoughts as you go about planning either an intimate space like this one, or perhaps something larger.

My client, Natalie Allen, lives in Brattleboro, Vermont (USDA Zone 4). Behind her gray two-and-a-half-story Victorian house is an 80-foot-deep, 30-foot-wide backyard. The back third of the yard is raised by a five-foot-high retaining wall through which steps climb to the upper level. Along the north side, between the back of the house and the stone wall, runs a stockade fence. Along the south side, an ell of the house stops six feet short of the stone wall to provide access to the backyard from the driveway on the other side of the ell. A 10-foot-wide deck connected to the back of the house stretches from the stockade fence to the ell.

To design this and many other gardens, I followed these eight steps.

1. ANALYZE THE SITE TO DETERMINE ITS QUALITIES

Once most of the snow was melted, in late March, I went to see the site of Natalie's garden for the first time. We sat on the deck bundled in coats, and looked closely at the backyard. Other than the flat lawn 30 feet wide and 50 feet deep, and a mature hemlock at the north end of the deck, there were no plants or features of any kind. Shade was dominant, caused by the ell to the south, the house to the west, the hemlock and trees along the neighbor's drive behind the stockade fence to the north, and the woods to the east. Sun was striking only a rectangle in the middle of her backyard. Even in midsummer, direct sun would only last from 10 a.m. until 4 p.m. Snow still lying in the shady sides and ends of the yard reminded us that Natalie would look out on a very snowy garden for five or six months of the year.

As we walked around, I noticed one unsightly view through the passageway to the driveway that would have to be screened. There were no distant or nearby views that were attractive enough to frame with shrubs or trees. The retaining wall was a good feature, but the cement steps that led through it to the upper level were cracked and leaning. They would have to be replaced with stones similar to those in the walls. The stone wall, as well as the ell of the house and the stockade fence, would form a light gray backdrop for plants. Finally, we both noted that there was a mature maple in the center of the woodland at the far end of the backyard. If saplings and under-brush were cleared from its trunk, it would form a strong focal point on the upper level.

We looked closely at the space for almost an hour, describing what we saw, seeing problems and, perhaps, inklings of solu-tions to them (none of which included specific plants—it was too early for that), and writing many of our thoughts down. Then we went inside for coffee. In the living room, looking out at the end-of-winter scene, we talked about the next important step in designing a garden.

2. DETERMINE WHAT ROLES THE GARDEN WILL PLAY IN YOUR LIFE

Natalie is retired and didn't have to consider the sandbox, laundry lines, basketball hoop, and general play space that are essential to a garden where children and dogs play. Her needs are different. She needed a garden that was an extension of her living room, a refined and vital place where she could entertain friends, be alone to read or do needlepoint, and retreat from the bustle of the town. Because she would sit in her living room during the winter looking out on the garden, shrubs and trees that would grow above the snow line would clearly be an important element of the design. Finally, she noted that she enjoys gardening but not to the point where she wants to be burdened by inordinate time spent weeding.

After coffee, we went from room to room looking out onto what would be the garden.

3. SEE THE GARDEN AS AN EXTENSION OF THE HOUSE

We talked about how Natalie lives in the house, and what implications that had for the design. She spends a lot of time in her study, for example, in the southwest corner of the house, looking out across the deck and underneath the hemlock in the northwest corner of the garden. That might suggest a need for many potted plants on the deck, and underplantings for the hemlock. From her bedroom on the second floor she looks down on the garden, so its overall shape would be important from there. But the place from which she would most often see the garden during the growing season was the deck, close to the foreground of the garden. Detail there, rather than mass, was called for.

We went back out to the deck and sat down again. There we noticed an alignment from the door to where we were sitting and on down the center of the lawn, up the steps in the retaining wall, to the large maple tree in the woodland at the back. That line would prove to be central to the organization of the garden. It was the axial line, and I later came to see many other lines develop in relation to it, for that line linked house to garden.

We had talked about a great deal that day, so we decided to mull over the day's thoughts before continuing. Over the next two weeks, I wrote down design ideas when they occurred to me. Before returning to Natalie's, I typed them all up so we had a record of our thoughts—all of them, good or bad. Two weeks later, when all the snow had melted in the backyard, I returned to take the next step.

Combine the step-by-step process used to create this backyard garden in southern Vermont with your knowledge of plants and your own property and you should be able to design your own landscape, one that includes trees, shrubs, vines, perennials, annuals, and vegetables.

4. MEASURE AND MAP

Measuring the site for a garden, and then drawing a large-scale plot-plan, is an important discipline. It forces you to look at your property objectively. With a 100-foot tape measure and a 24-by-36-inch sheet of paper taped to cardboard, Natalie and I measured the area to the nearest foot using a scale that would enable me to get the whole layout on the one sheet. In this case the scale was one-quarter inch to one foot.

We started by measuring the sides of the house, noting where doors and windows were along the walls and their height above the ground. Then I measured from the house to key points: outer boundaries first, then important inner points such as the stone wall, steps, and large maple tree. After measuring, I went around with a shovel to determine the nature of the soil, making notes on my rough map. I also photographed the garden with color transparency film.

5. Write out problems your design will have to solve

The act of drawing the scaled plot-plan helps me see patterns in the space. As a result, problems that I have to solve with the design begin to appear. For example:

- What elements would invite people to walk from the house or deck into the garden?
- What could be incorporated into the design to make the space appear to be larger than it actually was?
- What qualities of plants or stones could be used to create different moods and atmospheres within the limited space?
- How could the entranceway be treated as a garden in itself, as well as a passageway to the main garden?
- Since the garden was too small and shady for a full blooming schedule of sun-loving perennials throughout the growing season, should I choose one season and emphasize it? Should I then bring color into the garden the rest of the year with annuals, evergreens, and perennials that, like grasses, would dry and remain attractive throughout the winter?

Once I had written out these and other problems we had to solve with the design, we could look for solutions.

6. DESIGN SOLUTIONS

First, we wrote down some broad governing ideas for the design:

- Because shade is the dominant point in Natalie's garden, and Natalie had told me she's a "shade person," we decided to emphasize shade-loving plants with a lawn area in the sunny center.
- Because so many shade-loving perennials and shrubs bloom in the spring, that was the season we would emphasize.
- Since we also knew that the garden would have to be handsome in summer, fall, and winter, we had to make choices that would emphasize the interplay of foliage, texture, and growth habit.
- To increase the feeling of size in the garden and to draw Natalie and her guests into it, we decided to have stone paths somewhere, with a bench as their destination point.
- We wanted the paths to draw people past gatherings of plants, behind tall plants, under the branches of trees, close to intensely planted areas, thus creating a variety of moods and feelings.
- The shapes of the lawn and gardens would have to be in proportion to the overall area, and to one another.
- Natalie is an informal person, so we wanted to avoid the formality of symmetry.

Having made the general decisions that would govern my specific drawings, I put pencil to paper. First, I laid a sheet of tracing paper over the plot-plan and sketched broad areas of lawn or cultivated garden space. I began experimenting with the overall shapes of lawn as opposed to cultivated garden space.

Wanting to give the garden a focus, I drew lines roughly following the existing shade-sun demarcation, leaving room for a four-foot-wide garden along the ell, a 14-foot-wide lawn and a 12-foot-wide garden along the stockade fence. At the end of the lawn, I designed a semicircular garden with its center on the axial line. This area would act as a focal point at the end of the lawn, and be reinforced by the trunk of the maple tree 30 feet behind it.

When I was satisfied with the sketches of the lawn and garden spaces, I put another sheet of tracing paper over both the plot-plan and the lawn-and-cultivated-garden overlay to develop ideas about walkways and paths through those spaces. Then came the specifics of plants.

7. SELECT PLANTS

Having found some broad solutions to the main problems, I could decide on specific plants to reach specific solutions. I laid another sheet of tracing paper over the three sheets to start work on trees and shrubs. Next would come an overlay for perennials and annuals, and finally one for bulbs.

To select plants, I see them as solutions to problems. For example, Natalie would sit on the deck or the bench and be close to plants in that area. So I wanted those plants to form detailed and varied juxtapositions of growth habit, flower and foliage color, and leaf texture.

I began by choosing the larger plants: shrubs. First, I wanted one that would form a strong foreground right by the deck, yet mature in proportion to that intimate area. The soil could become dry in what was a sometimes breezeless backyard. It was in part a spring garden, and I wanted a deciduous plant that would give an open, airy look to the foreground and still offer a handsome growth habit in winter, seen from Natalie's living-room window. Many roads led me to *Fothergilla gardenii* as well as *Viburnum lantana*. Because I couldn't find a source for a *Fothergilla* of sufficient size, I chose *Viburnum lantana*.

Then I considered what perennials would complement the flowers and leaf texture and color of the viburnums, and each other. Eventually a foliage garden with spring bloom and a variety of heights and leaf forms emerged: *Primula japonica*, *Epimedium youngianum* and *rubrum*, *Hosta sieboldiana elegans*, *Bergenia cordifolia*, maidenhair and Christmas ferns, several kinds of astilbes, bloodroot, thalictrums. In some areas I worked with groups of five to seven plants to make firm and assertive statements, and also to plant thickly enough to shade the ground immediately, reducing Natalie's weeding.

After the shrub and perennial overlays, I started on the bulb overlay. The leaves of daffodils and tulips were too large to hide among the lower-growing foliage plants I had chosen, so I sketched in *Galanthus elwesii*, large-flowering crocuses, and *Leucojum aestivum* 'Gravetye'.

8. FINE-TUNE THE DESIGN WHEN PLANTING

The fine-tuning of any design takes place when the stones and plants are being put in the ground. You invariably make changes, for working with soil and plants helps you see the design more clearly and in detail. For example, when we were planting later that spring, we discovered that the soil was much more gravelly in places than we thought, so we had to shift the position of a white birch clump.

I originally designed fieldstone steps through the entrance from the driveway. But one day Natalie said she had large slate steps, some nearly three feet across, in her cellar so we used them instead. Those steps were much larger than originally drawn, so we needed fewer Christmas ferns on either side.

I haven't discussed the influence of budget on the overall design. At first Natalie and I ignored the constraints of money and time. We let our imaginations run free so that ideas flowed and the unusual and unexpected could develop. (We may yet put a pool and fountain in the semicircular garden.) Then we cut back according to budget.

If you follow a logical sequence and proceed with confidence, designing your own landscape can be a satisfying process and result in a most pleasing garden. This was attested to by Natalie and the guests at her first garden party the following spring.

2

UNDER THE EAVES

Those four- to eight-foot-wide bands of soil that run along under the eaves of our houses in the snowy parts of North America are difficult areas to plant. During the winter, snow builds up on the roof for a few days or weeks and then cascades down, snapping or crushing shrubs or small trees planted below.

Every spring we discover the damage and get our pruners out. When we're done, we've got misshapen yews or junipers, rhododendrons or mountain laurel, and we swear we'll make wooden covers for them next fall. And sure enough, come October, those wooden triangles begin to sprout up all across the northern tier of North America: two old shutters leaning against each other, two pieces of plywood hinged along the top with a strip of aluminum, or more elaborate, carpenter-constructed affairs that really do a job.

It doesn't have to be this way. Certainly, we don't want the front and back of our homes to look barren. But neither do we want to rely forever on the limiting Victorian notion of evergreens tight against the house, covered six months of the year with plywood.

One winter, I designed plantings around a 200-year-old house in nearby Putney, Vermont (Zone 4). Part of that design included the fully shaded east side of the house where for years snow had been sliding down off the eaves onto now-battered yews, mountain laurel, and rhododendrons. The other area included the south side of the house along the eaves of an ell where, in full sun, only one spirea at the corner and a lilac by the mud-room door had been planted decades ago.

As I worked on the design, I developed treatments for both areas, in keeping with the character of the new owners and their classic colonial home. But I kept wondering: How would other garden designers solve the snow problem? Answering this question took me on a fascinating exploration that taught me a lot about how we think about foundation planting in particular and garden design in general. I also learned about snow and how it differs as we move across the continent. In the process, I developed satisfying designs for the two problem areas I was faced with.

THE NATURE OF SNOW

First, let's take a look at the nature of snow across the U.S. and Canada. Hydrologists with the U.S. Weather Service quantify the wetness of snow with a ratio: the number of inches of snow it will take to produce one inch of water. The lower the ratio, the heavier the snow and the more damage it does to shrubs. For example, in New England, close to the Atlantic Ocean and not too mountainous, 10 inches of snow will usually produce one inch of water (10:1). Some early or late New England snows have a ratio as low as 6:1. Once snow is on a roof, the ratio drops even further by slow compaction as snow crystals collapse under their own weight, or are partially thawed by heat radiating through a poorly insulated roof. When that heavy snow drops onto mountain laurel, the shrub's brittle wood snaps.

A different situation prevails in the Pacific Northwest and the Rockies. Snow heavily laden with moisture (10:1 to 15:1) can sweep off the Pacific and drop on western Oregon and Washington. But as the wind carries the snow clouds over the Cascade mountain range, they get "wrung out," in the words of Steve Maleski, a meteorologist at the Fairbanks Museum in St. Johnsbury, Vermont. Then the snow clouds are pushed over the Rocky Mountains, where the colder temperatures at higher altitudes cause snow crystals to form a lacier, more open structure. This produces a drier snow with a higher snow-to-water ratio. By the time the storm off the Pacific reaches the eastern Rockies, the ratio might be as high as 50:1. That's a very powdery snow that will cause no damage at all to shrubs. The windier conditions in that area also mean that snow is often blown off roofs, sometimes settling around shrubs and protecting them.

Usually, the further inland you get from either coast, the higher the ratio, Maleski notes. An exception is snow from storms that travel from the Gulf of Mexico up the Mississippi River. Snow in the Midwest averages 10:1 to 12:1. The same ratio is true for the high plains area (eastern Montana, Wyoming, Nebraska, and the western Dakotas) in early fall and late spring, though mid-winter snow is more powdery there.

ARCHITECTURAL SOLUTIONS

In the Rockies, where the snow is generally light and airy, designers often look to the roof to solve what they regard as a minor problem of snow cascading down on foundation plants. Bruce Lutz, a landscape designer working in an architectural firm in Kalispell, Montana, tells me that roof cleats are a typical solution there. These are metal bars affixed across roofs to hold snow in place. This isn't a practical solution for the East or Midwest, however, because the more frequent freeze-thaw cycle would cause a weighty ice build-up that could creep in under roofing materials and cause damage.

Lutz also suggests that cedar shakes and asphalt shingles, because of their texture, tend to hold snow in place better than metal or slate roofs, especially in combination with a "cold roof." Such a roof is kept cold with venting systems that create a gap between the roof itself and the insulation for the ceiling of the upper story. This gap helps the roof stay cold, which prevents melting and thus keeps the snow on it.

A gently sloping roof helps too, as do roofs that overhang as far as four to six feet. This solution is possible on the eastern slope of the Rockies where, again, the snow is lighter and is often blown away. The hefty overhang, however, creates another problem. If the soil underneath is to be planted, it has to be fitted with drip irrigation, or plants won't get sufficient moisture.

But many of us have metal or slate roofs, or other kinds that, for one reason or another, simply don't hold the snow. In that case, we need to rethink our whole concept of foundation planting. If we do, a whole new set of plants can enter into the gardens we design for the eave sides of our homes.

Get rid of straight lines

I started to rethink foundation planting with Margaret Hensel, a garden designer and writer who works in western Massachusetts. What we realized is that to redefine that planting area, you have to be willing to let go of the straight line. Think of all the foundation plantings you've seen. They're typically within a four- to eight-foot-wide bed whose front edge probably runs parallel to the house. I thought about the old foundation planting at the Putney property I was working on. Sure enough, the shrubs were in a straight-edged bed, six feet out and parallel to the front of the house.

Let go of that tight straight line, Hensel said, and instead let a curved line flow out 6 to 10 feet into what is typically lawn. If you set shrubs and perennials informally within that space, you can bring new life to foundation plantings.

We took a closer look at a bird's-eye-view drawing I had made of the existing plantings on the eave side of the Putney house. I knew that the mature mountain laurel on the left and the mature rhododendron on the right were battered at the back, three or four feet from the house, but their front sides were in quite good shape. Because they were such large specimens, and not easily replaced, we decided, with the encouragement of my clients, to leave them in place, but to remove the more battered yews nearer the house.

We then considered how the front edge of the garden, bisected by stepping stones to the front door, would run. To make the entrance more informal, we tried a variety of curving lines that swept from the stepping stones out into the lawn six or eight feet and then back and, still four feet out from the house, right around each corner. The curves were slightly different on each side to avoid the static feeling that results from symmetry.

Once we got the lines right, we looked at how to plant the spaces. Hensel suggested planting royal ferns (*Osmunda regalis*) in informal drifts behind the two existing evergreens. They would hide the backs of the two mature shrubs and form a backdrop for them as well as for smaller drifts of *Anemone hupehensis* we decided to plant beside the evergreens. She suggested planting the foreground of the two beds with three varying-sized drifts of *Vinca minor* 'Bowles', a deep-blue-flowering cultivar, and the white-flowering 'Gertrude Jekyll'. Two drifts of the shade-tolerant, needled evergreen groundcover, creeping false cypress (*Microbiota decussata*), among the vinca would add a contrasting texture and color. Furthermore, being a low shrub, snow could fall on it and the vinca and cause no damage.

Landscaping the eave side of your house can be a problem, especially if you live in northern North America where snow cascades down, snapping branches off your favorite shrubs. There are many design alternatives and plant choices that will help you improve your foundation planting.

Had the broadleaved evergreens not been there, we would have gone on to explore alternative evergreens to provide year-round interest in our wintry area of the country. We might have considered three or four spreading yews (*Taxus densiformis*) or hollies (*Ilex meserve* 'China Boy' or 'Girl') on either side of the front doorway. Behind them, where the snow would fall, we could have considered fall-blooming *Anemone hupehensis*, Ostrich ferns (*Matteuccia struthiopteris*), or royal ferns. In front, we could have planted Wilson's rhododendron (*Rhododendron × wilsonii*), which could be edged along the front with the two spring-blooming vincas, ajuga, or pachysandra. The shrubs and groundcovers would be planted outside the snowdrop line, with perennials that die back in the autumn between the outer edge of that line and the house.

The curving line that swept around the southeast corner of the house linked up with the full-sun area on the southern eave side of the house, in a place where I knew my clients wanted a bluestone terrace and associated plantings. I had previously designed this with snow in mind. The terrace would be in two sections, right up to the foundation, leaving one planting space near the house for perennials that would give summer interest yet die down in the winter. The bluestone would take the shock of the falling snow, and during the summer potted plants or lawn furniture could be set out against the foundation to soften it. I also designed a simple grape arbor to shade a portion of the terrace.

What plantings I did suggest were at the outer corners of the terrace, where they would be well out of the way of cascading snow. To provide some shade, yet at the same time remain relatively open for a view into a stone-wall-enclosed garden across the lawn, I suggested the Whitespire Japanese white birch (*Betula platyphylla japonica* 'Whitespire'), underplanted with a low spreading juniper (*Juniperus horizontalis* 'Hughes'), in turn interplanted with one or two clumps of fountain grass (*Pennisetum alopecuroides*). This combination of deciduous tree, evergreen groundcover, and perennial grass would provide year-round interest, especially given that the grass dies to a beige-brown and remains relatively intact for two or three months into the winter.

MORE PLANT CHOICES

Here's some more advice on plant choices, including suggestions from Del Cook of Salt Lake City, Utah, and Tom Hopps of Camden, Maine.

- Choose plant material that's not brittle. *Hypericum prolificum*, for example, under the eaves of my barn withstands any amount of snow and ice on it; more brittle tree peonies would snap. *Pinus mugho* is also resilient, as are junipers and yews.
- Choose shrubs such as hydrangeas, *Buddleia davidii*, and *Clethra alnifolia* that bloom only on new wood. If branches are snapped, the plant will still flower on that season's wood. A rule of thumb is that any shrub that blooms after July 1 blooms on new wood.
- Choose shrubs that, like many junipers, *Mahonia aquifolium*, and *Leucothoe fontanesiana*, are prostrate in their growth habit and won't be damaged the way upright plants would be.
- Choose tough perennials such as ferns, hostas, New England asters, and countless others that will die to ground level and thus be out of harm's way. (There are also many plants that will suffer under the weight and suffocation of the snow and ice. *Coreopsis lanceolata*, *Oenothera biennis*, and *Campanula persicifolia* are a few examples.)
- Choose large perennials that can produce a shrub-like effect: herbaceous peonies, large-leaved hostas, ostrich fern, *Baptisia australis*. These die back in autumn and remain below ground and out of harm's way throughout the winter.

MECHANICAL AND OTHER SOLUTIONS

Tom Hopps also suggests these mechanical solutions (as alternatives to the wooden teepees) for supporting or protecting existing foundation plantings.

- Encircle the upright limbs of yews or junipers with green nursery twine to strengthen them against snow-drop.
- To make vertical shrubbery such as *Enkianthus campanulatus*, shadblow (*Amelanchier canadensis*), and lilacs more resistant to snowdrop, drive three or four stakes around the shrub and tie major stems to these stakes at several different heights.
- Where evergreen boughs are in ample supply, work them generously into rhododendrons, mountain laurel, and other evergreen shrubs to bolster the shrub and reduce the risk of snow damage.

Other solutions suggested by all the designers I've cited:

- Design shrub planting five to six feet out from the foundation itself. Cover that open band of soil with permeable, woven (not sheet), black plastic ground cloth, in turn covered with bark mulch.
- If a house is not a Victorian on a high foundation, the need for foundation planting is lessened. Many modern houses sit snug to the ground, so you can plant primarily at the corners or well away from the house where the plants can be seen from the inside as well.
- Colonial homes rarely if ever had foundation plantings. Instead, the owners planted little more than a lilac at each corner of the front of the house, just out of reach of cascading snow. Otherwise, the front was frequently left plain.
- For a house close to a street or road, run a four- or five-foot-wide stone walkway along the side of the house, and then plant a hedge—lilac, peony, yew, baptisia— between the road and the outer edge of the walkway. The snow lands on the stone, and not on the shrubs or perennials. Salt-tolerant hedges can be planted, for example, with any of the following: Pfitzer junipers, privet, Japanese barberry, *Euonymus alatus compacta*, Vanhoutte spirea, weigela, yews, arborvitaes, hemlock, forsythia.

- For a house 40 or more feet back from a street, turn the whole area between house and street into a garden and have no lawn at all. For full-sun sites, interplant broad sweeps of grasses, junipers, sedums, and *Rudbeckia goldsturm*, following the example of the much publicized work of Ohme-van Sweden, a landscape design firm in Washington, D.C.

Getting rid of the invariably unsatisfying lawn under trees between the house and street has worked well for several of my clients. You can then transplant existing foundation plants and add others to create a woodland garden where the lawn was. For example, for clients in Sudbury, Massachusetts, I took up a thin and struggling lawn under 15 or so mature oaks in the 50-foot area between house and street. We then rolled large boulders into various places where groups of shrubs would be, and laid a fieldstone walkway that curved from the driveway and among the trees and boulders to the front door. Once this heavy work was done, I planted groups of rhododendrons, azaleas, *Pieris japonica*, oak-leaved hydrangea (*Hydrangea quercifolia*), and *Enkianthus campanulatus* among the trees and near the boulders. Interplanted with the shrub groupings were Christmas ferns (*Polystichum acrostichoides*) and large-leaved hostas, themselves interplanted with hundreds of large-flowering crocuses.

Change isn't easy. We have lived with, and struggled with the whole notion of foundation planting ever since the Victorians wanted to cover up their particularly obtrusive foundations. By letting go of their tight, linear solutions, by letting go of even a part of the sacrosanct front lawn, we might be able to redefine, in modern terms, how we can enliven plantings near our homes, especially under the eaves.

3 🌿

THE WINTER GARDEN

From November to April, snow covers everything but trees, shrubs, and the tops of stone walls here in our southern Vermont garden. Four years ago, when my wife, Mary, and I purchased this property, with its long-neglected grounds, we looked out from the kitchen and across the drive to the tangled black branches of wild plum trees. From my desk in the study I saw an acre of snow-covered lawn ending in two unpruned apple trees and a row of black locusts overgrown by saplings.

But a garden in winter—even in a cold climate like ours—need not be so bleak, so colorless, or such a confusion of growth. In winter the texture of plants, the sculptural lines of bare branches, the mass of evergreen trees and shrubs, and more subtle shades of color can become sources of much beauty. There are plants that will add reds, yellows, grays, greens, and blues to the winter landscape with their fruits, bark, foliage, and even flowers.

To plan a winter garden, first consider what areas to develop. Mary and I went from room to room inspecting views and discovered that the most important ones were from the kitchen, the study, and the living room. Outside, we considered what we saw as we came up the drive or walked out to the shed. We largely disregarded those areas of our property that we rarely saw throughout the winter.

We then studied the existing trees and shrubs around our 200-year-old farmhouse. A winter garden must be well groomed because the outlines and forms of trees and shrubs are so prominent. So before doing any new planting we thinned and pruned.

I "released" the stand of black locusts at the end of the lawn by cutting out the leggy young maple, black-cherry, and ash trees that had insinuated themselves into the locust row. What

was a confused tangle of growth is now a row of spare silhou-
ettes against the winter sky. I also pruned the apple trees, first
removing the interior branches, water sprouts, and deadwood,
then thinning the outer branches to form an umbrella-shaped
canopy of limbs. From the thicket of flowering plums across
from the kitchen window I pruned out the deadwood and
interior branches that get very little sunlight during the growing season. Now their branches look more swirling than chaotic, making an interesting foil to the ordered lines of a nearby
stone wall and a row of 'Bosc' pear trees.

LINE AND COLOR

Weeping trees and shrubs are especially attractive to anyone
who wants to emphasize line in the winter landscape — whether
on a city terrace, a suburban lot, or a rural garden. *Cedrus
atlantica* (Zone 7) is available in a weeping form, as is the
Siberian pea tree (*Caragana arborescens* var. *pendula*, Zone 2),
weeping Camperdown elm (a hybrid of *Ulmus carpinifolia* and
U. glabra, hardy to Zone 4), and weeping mulberry (*Murus alba*
'Pendula', Zone 5).

Pruning and form are questions of line. We wanted color too,
for it's the reds and yellows and silvery greens that can pull you
through the late-February blues. We turned first to trees because they live longer than shrubs and dominate them in design. Crab apples particularly interested us because of their
bright, persistent fruits.

Malus × *zumi* var. *calocarpa* is an especially good crab. Hardy
to minus 30 degrees Fahrenheit, this cultivar holds its brilliant-
red apples well into February or March in our Zone 4 garden.
It's resistant to scab, fire blight, and rust. We thought it would
also contrast nicely with the silver boards of our old shed.

Hawthorns also carry fruit well into winter, though most are
hardy only to Zone 5. *Crataegus viridis* 'Winter King' is one of
the better cultivars. It remains laden with shiny red fruits until
early spring. Another hawthorn useful to gardeners farther
south is *C. brachyacantha*, from the Gulf Coast. With its dark-
blue fruits *C. brachyacantha* should always be planted near
walkways or close to important vantage points because the
color doesn't carry far.

Evergreen hollies carry red or yellow berries throughout the winter. Plants that offer reds or yellows can be planted farther away from the house because those colors can be seen from a greater distance. The deciduous *Ilex verticillata*, commonly known as winterberry, is native to our area. Just down the road is a wet, shady spot where several winterberries grow in front of a hemlock grove. In deep winter that corner of the wood is a study in black stems, red berries, green needles, and white snow.

Bark can also add subtle color to a snow bound, leafless garden. The sycamore (*Platanus* × *acerifolia*, Zone 5), for example, has a handsome, mottled bark. Cream colored when young, it flakes off mature trees in large patches to reveal a yellow inner layer. We already have a mature birch on our property. I may plant a few hemlocks behind it to accent its clean white bark and add green to that area in winter. Red osier (*Cornus sericea*, Zone 3) provides red bark in winter. This and its golden-twigged relative *C. sericea* 'Flaviramea' favor wet, marshy soil. Both spread vigorously and so may be best planted in clumps away from other cultivated plants. To keep these shrubs' young, brightly colored wood coming, prune back the older wood each spring.

Winter color from flowers is something gardeners in the North rarely think about. But two cultivars of witch hazel developed by the Arnold Arboretum add bloom in Zones 5 through 9. Grown best at the edge of a woodland, *Hamamelis* × *intermedia* 'Arnold Promise' blooms on late-winter days. Its clear-yellow petals unwind like tiny springs in the morning sun and rewind at sunset. Crimson 'Diana' flowers a bit earlier than 'Arnold Promise'. Heaths and heathers also throw orange-red and pink flowers (Zones 5-8). Even the Christmas rose (*Helleborus niger*) can add fresh blooms and evergreen foliage to the winter garden. I have a friend in Walpole, New Hampshire (Zone 4), who nurses his along from year to year.

EVERGREENS

Evergreens can add color, texture, and mass to the winter garden. Look closely at the many hues of needled and broad-leaved evergreens and you will find numerous shades of

For a garden that looks good year-round, combine broadleaved and needled evergreens with deciduous shrubs and trees that have interesting bark, fruits, or berries, and with perennials that hold their form throughout the winter. The result can be a very stimulating picture.

yellows, silver-blues, and greens. Many that are green during the growing season turn to shades of purple in the winter. The foliage of *Andromeda glaucophylla* (Zone 3) turns a plum color with a silver sheen; the gray-green foliage of *Juniperus horizontalis* 'Douglasii' (Zone 4) turns a purplish blue.

We took advantage of this changing color, as well as a variety of plant habit, when we planted several 'P.J.M. Balta' rhododendrons in front of the native, and more leggy, *Kalmia latifolia* mountain laurels that we had planted under the flowering plum trees. During the growing season the compact, white-flowering 'Balta' hides the bases of the laurels and contrasts nicely with their more open and taller growth. During the winter the rounded, purple foliage of the 'Balta' turns bronze, while the lance-shaped mountain-laurel leaves remain deep green, providing a handsome backdrop.

To be certain that these evergreens can survive the winter here, we plant them where sunlight will be broken by the deciduous trees overhead. I also surround the plants with a four- to five-inch-thick mulch of pine needles each fall and water them well before the ground freezes to assure these continually transpiring plants plenty of moisture.

Deciduous trees and shrubs can also form an important contrast with evergreen shrubs in the winter garden. We are considering, for example, interplanting laurel and rhododendrons with azaleas and enkianthus. The growth habits of the four plants will provide a variety of line, color, and density. To tie the whole picture together we may plant ground-hugging leucothoe, with its bronzy-green winter foliage, along the front of this shrub border. The lines of the deciduous azalea and enkianthus branches will lighten the mass of broad-leaved evergreens. The varying textures and colors of the leaves should make for a rich composition. These ideas can be applied to hedges as well. Lawrence Johnston interplanted hollies, yew, box, and beech in his famous garden at Hidcote Manor, to make what he called a tapestry hedge that is strikingly different in summer and winter.

Needled evergreens further broaden the spectrum of colors, growth habits, and textures in the winter garden—and their branches hold snow better for a nicer contrast of green and white. For gardeners in Zones 7 and south, the blue Atlas cedar

(*Cedrus atlantica* 'Glauca') adds silvery-blue tones with its short, stiff needles, while *Thuja occidentalis* 'Lutea' (Zone 3) and *Chamaecyparis pisifera* (Zone 5) add yellow-greens as well as softer textures that result from their fern-like, flattened foliage.

Friends who live in New York City (Zone 7) recently asked me what evergreens they might use as container plants for their terrace in winter. One can grow a broad variety of slow-growing evergreens in wooden containers that are at least 18 by 18 inches. The globe-shaped white pine *Pinus strobus* 'Nana', with its long, soft needles, or the slow-growing Colorado blue spruce *Picea pungens* 'Compacta', with its conical shape and stiff, short needles, are two good examples. Choose slow-growing or dwarf plants with varying types and colors of needles as well as different growth habits and you will add much vitality to your winter view.

In making an interesting winter garden, try to choose plants that are attractive in other seasons as well. We enjoy the red twigs of highbush blueberry against the snow almost as much as its fruit in July. Adding trees, shrubs, and even hardy perennials to the garden enlivens the views from windows and walkways throughout the year. These plants are in turn animated by winter's agents of change—wind, snow, frost, gleaming sunlight, bright blue skies, and visiting animals. Frost glistens on red barberries, and snow accents the shrub's shape. A blue jay alights on a white birch. Overnight, alder twigs turn white with frost; sunlight turns them back to black.

4

CREATING A
WOODLAND PATH

A woodland path, whether it leads through a small copse of trees or into acres of woods, has the power to create a mood that is unlike any other in the garden. While flower borders in full sun stimulate the eye with bright colors, the woodland path in dappled shade cools and calms with subtler ones. While the rock garden can be intense and studied, the woodland path is relaxed and natural. While the lawn is sunny and open, the woodland path is shaded and enclosed. It's a private area in our larger garden that offers a cool and contemplative respite.

To create a woodland path, you can simply clear a short walk that winds through a copse following the path of least resistance, or create a longer walk through acres of woodland along which shrubs and perennials can be planted. You can also spread the project over many years, clearing the path first and planting areas along it as the years go by.

The woodland path offers the potential for remarkable variety. At one moment it can lead you to a mossy boulder that's a natural garden in itself and the next moment you're looking through cleared woods to an expansive view of distant hills. One moment you're in full shade and the next in a pool of light. In spring, azaleas, rhododendrons, and other shade-tolerant perennials that can be planted along the path stand out as areas of drama and color. In summer the path is shaded and cool, with foliage creating an interplay of greens and textures. In autumn brilliant red, orange, and yellow leaves hold overhead for a week or two and then fall to the ground. In winter, the woodland path leads walkers or cross-country skiers past evergreens, over a white carpet of snow, and among gray and black tree trunks with their tracery of limbs against the blue sky.

You don't need to own acres of woodland to create and enjoy a woodland path. My wife and I created one in a small copse. At the edge we planted shrubs to enclose the woods, and through the length of it we ran a path between plantings of perennials, ferns, and smaller shrubs. Other woodland paths can pass through a narrow band of woods that separate one building or garden space from another. Others can be cleared paths through a half-acre or more of woodland with unusual trees or shrubs, clearings, streams, or views, as yet unplanted and "unimproved" by us. Whatever the approach, a path through the woods leads to an increased appreciation of the beauty and peace inherent in woodland.

Three paths I've created provide examples of the variety possible in woodland walks. The smallest is located at the end of my own property in a 30-by-70-foot area of deciduous trees bordered by a section of lawn to the north and a stone wall and meadow to the south. The second was created within five acres of generally flat and mature beech, maple, and oak woodland owned by Phil and Amy Geier in southern Vermont. More woodland surrounded the five acres, at one edge of which was their home. The third site was through a 100-foot-wide strip of steeply sloping woodland of mature white birch, hemlock, and maple that separated a client's guest house below from the main house on a cleared New Hampshire hilltop.

DESIGN GUIDELINES

A woodland walk is best designed among the trees, not on paper. That's because natural contours and rocks, trees, and water—that is, points of interest in the woods—provide clues to the direction of the most varied path.

The first clues come from existing plants and rocks. In the five acres of woodland near the Geiers' home, for example, were three 20- to 30-foot-long lichen- and moss-covered rock outcroppings with ferns growing here and there in crevices. Several closely growing pairs or clumps of mature beech trees suggested gateways or passageways. Rotted stumps that were hosts to natural miniature gardens of mosses, ferns, and spleenworts also gave us clues to the direction the path should take.

Another clue about direction comes from existing or potential views, such as the view in the New Hampshire path over a stone wall and up through beech and hemlocks to the eighteenth-century home on the hilltop.

A third source of clues are pockets or areas of soil that are relatively root-free, where new plants can easily be introduced. If you're lucky, you'll find a variety of soil conditions in those areas, enabling you to plant different kinds of shade-tolerant shrubs and perennials.

As I walk through larger four- or five-acre woodlands looking for these points of interest, I carry a roll of bright forester's tape to mark the trees, rock outcroppings, and other points of interest. I tie the tape to four-foot stakes or to nearby branches so I can see the points from a distance. Once I've explored all the woodland, I go back to the outside of the woods to consider the starting and ending points of the path. The two ends can be suggested by a relationship to a door in the house, an existing pathway, areas of lawn, or breaks that exist or can be made in stone walls.

Knowing where the landmarks are in the woods, and where the ends of a path will be, I wander through the woods looking for patterns in tapes tied to trees or stakes. That helps me determine the best direction for the path. You have to be careful not to slavishly follow the perimeter of the property, for in thinking that way you can end up with too many stretches of long, straight path. Curves and turns add suspense, and draw us on.

Though direction is one way to vary a path, so is dimension. The trunks or branches of trees and shrubs on either side can funnel closer and closer and then suddenly widen. Tree branches above can also be left or pruned to create different effects. In the Geiers' path, for example, I used an extension ladder to high-prune one group of 10 or more beeches up 30 feet, creating a lofty canopy in that area. At other places, I pruned limbs to make an arch as low as seven or eight feet over the path to create an intimate feeling as one walked or skiied under the arch.

You can create a woodland walk whether you have acres of trees or just a small copse in the backyard. Using a few design principles, you'll discover how simple it is to make one, and how rich and varied even the shortest of paths can be.

Light is another variable: one moment you're in full shade, the next in a pool of sunshine. Distance between you and a point of interest is yet another source of variety. Passing within a few feet of an intimately planted rock outcropping you might come around a turn in the path to find yourself in a 15-foot-wide clearing, at the end of which is a dramatic view through

the woods. And a path should offer a destination such as a
bench or sitting area.

THREE PHASES OF WORK

Once a path is roughly laid out with tapes, I start clearing it at
one end, dividing the work into three phases. First, I work its
length, removing undergrowth and saplings—that is, trees that
either can be uprooted by hand and shovel or cut with a
handsaw. In mature, open forest, such as the Geiers', it took
only six hours to clear a path through five acres, scattering the
brush in the woodland.

Next, if necessary, I work the length of the path with a chain
saw, taking out larger trees that either block the smooth running of the path, block views, or confuse the image of more
satisfying trees. Clearing small trees from the base of a magnifi-
cent birch in the New Hampshire path was like drawing a
curtain back to reveal a vast sculpture.

Finally, I make a third pass to fine-tune the image with
pruning shears and a handsaw. In the Geiers' woods, I opened
a line of view between the trunks of several 150-year-old maple
trees to open a view into a sheep meadow. At another point, I
cut a "window" in saplings to frame a view of a seasonal
freshet. We also cut small saplings from along a mossy old
stone wall, leaving the tumbled stones just as they were. Because the Geiers' woods offered so many varied woodland
images, that six-hour process completed their woodland path.
Someday we might add plantings. But for now, the path looks
wonderful just as it is.

Because there was only a minimum of inherent interest in the
New Hampshire path or ours, the next step in both those cases
was to decide where to introduce additional plants to provide
areas of surprise or intimacy, screening or drama. To be most
satisfactory, new plantings need to look as natural as possible.
To do this, I locate new plantings in relation to existing landmarks: the entrance to paths, or near boulders, rock outcroppings, or a bench.

PREPARING THE SOIL

When additional plants are necessary, soil preparation is the
next step. I've often found that woodland soil has been ex-

hausted by ferocious competition among existing trees and shrubs for water and nutrients. In such cases, I find areas where the ground isn't too rooty and excavate the existing soil to a depth of a foot or more, then replace it with equal parts of topsoil, compost, and peat.

For relatively root-free areas where the soil isn't wholly depleted but needs enrichment, I fork the soil and spread amendments on the area (for clayey soil, equal parts sand, compost, and topsoil; for sandy soil, equal amounts of topsoil and compost) and then fork them in. I've also planted on top of rooty woodland soil rather than in it, by spreading an 8- to 10-inch layer of a soil mixture as mentioned above and then planting in that soil. Particularly tough plants—hostas, the Christmas fern (*Polystichum acrostichoides*), maidenhair fern (*Adiantum pedatum*), or the woodsias are just a few—can get a good hold this way before the surface roots of more aggressive trees get into the soil.

Plants to introduce along a woodland path should complement the beauty of the natural woodland. In the New Hampshire path, for example, we wanted spring-blooming woodland plants, so we planted shrubs and hardy perennials that could be found growing wild in the area. For example, we planted several witch hazels (*Hamamelis mollis*) and winterberry (*Ilex verticillata*) on the inside or outside of the curves or at the entrances and then underplanted them with a combination of trilliums, bloodroot, trout lilies, Christmas ferns, and *Tiarella cordifolia*. It was a simple planting that two of us finished in a morning, and the path was complete.

PLANTS FOR THE WOODLAND

Because our own home woodland needed many plants to become satisfying, my wife and I had a much larger job on our hands, and the garden will take several years to mature. But that process is part of the pleasure. First we planted an informal screen of deciduous shrubs to visually separate the lawn area from the walkway through the length of the woodland copse. We planted *Viburnum dentata, Viburnum lantana, Hamamelis* × *intermedia* 'Diana', *Clethra alnifolia*, and *Enkianthus campanulatus*, all in deep, compost-enriched soil, leaving room to plant both sides of this "screen."

To mark one entrance, I set two seven-foot granite fenceposts on either side of the first large stepping stones that formed the walkway. I planted *Hosta* 'Frances Williams' around one, interplanted with the daffodil 'Louise de Coligny'. Near the other upright stone, I put a young *Magnolia stellata*, underplanted with *Bellis perennis*, *Phlox stolonifera* 'Bruce's White' and 'Blue Ridge', and *Dicentra formosa* 'Alba' in the midst of which rose the relatively upright *Hosta* 'Krossa Regal'.

Along the stone walkway I gathered combinations of other perennial plants: *Bergenia cordifolia*, *Hosta sieboldiana* 'Elegans', *Epimedium youngianum niveum* and *rubrum*, *Pulmonaria angustifolia*, *Sanguinaria canadensis* 'Flore pleno', *Dicentra spectabilis* and its 'Alba' form, as well as the blue *Phlox divaricata*. At the other end of the walkway, we planted a young *Stewartia pseudocamellia* on one side and another granite fencepost on the other, using royal ferns (*Osmunda regalis*), *Phlox stolonifera*, *Bergenia cordifolia*, and *Hosta grandiflora* for groundcovers.

Because our woodland path was so small, we were able to set stepping stones the length of it. The problem of covering considerably longer paths is more easily solved. Let autumn leaves fall on the path. They form a good mulch and an attractive, natural covering.

Maintenance of a path is simple. Each autumn, shoots that arise from stumps of trees or saplings have to be cut back, as do branches that have grown into the walkway. Planted areas can be mulched with two to four inches of compost or manure. In the spring, a 10-10-10 fertilizer can be spread on those same areas. Only a minimum of weeding seems necessary in a shaded or woodland setting.

A well-designed and well-planted path provides years, even decades, of pleasure as well as a quiet and introspective place for contemplation. Yet at the same time it's dynamic and continuously changing: with the weather, with the seasons, with passing daylight, and with the growth and change in plants. And because of these changes, the mood and feeling in a woodland walk are always different, thus ever engaging our imagination.

TREES, SHRUBS, and VINES

Once you've developed an overall design for your landscape, the first plants to locate in the design are the larger ones: trees, shrubs, and, in some cases, vines. Several of the plants discussed in this section were subjects for the "Native American" series in Horticulture. *Other chapters I've included should help you expand your choice of larger plants for your garden. Whichever of these trees, shrubs, or vines you choose, these chapters will help you to see how to combine them in satisfying ways with herbaceous plants such as bulbs or perennials.*

5

YELLOWWOOD

In May 1855, Reverend Frederick Newman Knapp of Walpole, New Hampshire, wanted to honor his bride, Lucia Alden. He planted a yellowwood tree that is still flourishing more than a century later.

Perhaps Reverend Knapp planted the yellowwood for the same reasons my wife and I did a few years ago. It's very hardy, yet beautiful, and many experts regard it as the foremost native American flowering shade tree. Indigenous to the mountains of North Carolina, Kentucky, Tennessee, and Arkansas, it flourishes across nearly all of America (Zones 3-8).

The yellowwood (*Cladrastis lutea*) is easily transplanted in well-drained soil. It has yellow heartwood (*lutea* means "yellow" in Greek) and its smooth, gray bark is reminiscent of, but more luminous than, the beech tree. Typically the trunk separates into several main stems four to six feet above ground level. At maturity it forms a 40-foot-tall, dome-shaped crown with an open growth habit. This makes it an excellent medium-sized tree for even small properties.

In mid May in Zone 4 the flower and leaf buds begin to break simultaneously. By late May or early June the tree can be covered with a cascade of fragrant wisteria-like, pure white blossoms whose individual florets resemble pea blossoms. (*Cladrastis* belongs to the pea family, Leguminosae.) Dense layers of dark-green compound leaves form their background.

Flowering, which lasts about two weeks but doesn't begin until the tree is 12 to 18 feet tall, tends to be irregular, partly because the opening flower buds are susceptible to late spring frosts. In the autumn, the leaves turn a delicate clear yellow, adding a glow to the garden.

The yellowwood's deep root system has allowed us to plant perennials beneath it without fear of root competition, a real

Regarded by many as the foremost native American flowering tree, yellowwood makes a superior specimen tree all by itself in an open area of your lawn. You can also underplant it with a combination of daylilies and ferns, in turn underplanted with miniature spring bulbs.

problem with such shade trees as maples and beeches. Day-lilies are the dominant plant for now, but as our tree grows older and casts a larger shadow, we could underplant it with shade-tolerant perennials such as hostas, epimediums, bergenias, sweet woodruff, maidenhair ferns, pulmonarias, and primulas as well as smaller shade-tolerant shrubs—daphne, kerria, leucothoe, and pieris, for example. Groundcovers like vinca, ajuga, and pachysandra would do nicely. A friend of ours removed the lower limbs of his yellowwood one late fall (spring pruning causes severe sap bleeding) to let more light in under the tree. He then underplanted it with a perennial-annual bed. Like all members of the pea family, the yellow-wood fixes atmospheric nitrogen, thus contributing to the health of underplantings.

The yellowwood grows one or two feet a year and is virtually free of pests and diseases. Even gypsy moths and canker worms shun it. But the yellowwood is not without its problems. Its wood is brittle, and the crotches that form where the trunk divides into several main branches can be narrow. This not only weakens the tree but also makes it susceptible to a fatal vascular disease. The tree's generic name, *Cladrastis*, implies this problem. The word is derived from two Greek roots: *klados*, meaning "branch," and *thraustos*, meaning "fragile." Cabling trees that appear to have weak crotches can help solve this problem. Or if you are buying young trees, select those with the broadest crotches.

Henry Francis and his wife, who have lived in the Knapp house for the past 20 years, tell me that when the old yellow-wood has bloomed profusely (1975 and 1982) they've been able to gather many seedlings the following spring. Over the years they've given seedlings away to friends and neighbors, carrying on the celebration of the yellowwood tree that Reverend Knapp started in 1855.

6 🌼

SHADBLOW

A simple, clean growth habit, refined foliage, delicate flowers, edible fruit, cold hardiness, and disease and pest resistance — it's a rare plant that combines all of these attributes. But shadblow (*Amelanchier canadensis*, sometimes confused with *A. arborea*) is just such a plant.

This erect, often multistemmed 10- to 15-foot shrub is one of the first to flower in the wild (it was given its common name by early settlers who noted that it bloomed when the shad were spawning). In my garden the blooms appear in late April or early May. Delicate, pure-white florets form upright racemes at the tips of airy, smooth, gray branches, creating a wispy, billowy effect. The young leaves, which are just beginning to emerge when the shrub is in bloom, are covered on both sides with short, densely packed hairs that give the shrub a silvery appearance and the "downy" in another common name, downy serviceberry. (The name "serviceberry" comes from colonial times. When this shrub bloomed the soil had thawed enough to hold a burial service for those who had died during the winter.)

About a month after the fleeting bloom is over, the leaves have matured to finely proportioned one- to two-inch ovals and edible fruits have developed. (The cultivar 'Success', hybridized from the smaller, related species *A. alnifolia*, carries especially abundant fruit.) By early June these fruits — somewhat bland versions of blueberries, and just as versatile in cooking — have ripened. (Thus the common name "Juneberry" in the South.)

In autumn the shadblow's yellow or bright-red leaves fall to expose a smooth, light-gray tracery of branches with reddish buds along the stems. These budded limbs lend a satisfying dimension to the winter garden, especially if the shrub is near the house.

Cold hardiness is another of shadblow's worthy traits. Indeed, *A. canadensis* is the most hardy member of its genus. Its native North American range implies its toughness and adaptability, for this shrub grows in moist, sometimes wet soils from Maine to Georgia and as far west as Louisiana, Iowa, and Missouri (Zones 3-8). In the garden its range is broad too—with sufficient moisture it can be planted almost anywhere between the house and deep woods.

As for pests and diseases, shadblow is generally trouble-free in the Northeast. In warmer, drier parts of the country, however, it can be susceptible to the troubles common to members of the rose family—namely, spider mites, scale, and fire blight. These problems can be controlled without difficulty in most cases. Remember that locally grown plants will adapt and perform best.

The shadblow's versatility is perhaps best illustrated by noting some successful planting combinations that can be made with it. Francis Rohr, a fellow Vermont gardener, planted a shadblow at the southeast corner of his home some 20 years ago. He pruned all but one trunk from the original plant, thus training it into a small tree. The white clapboards of the house form a nice backdrop for the smooth, gray trunk and branches, while *Epimedium rubrum* forms a groundcover. Other plantings at the base of a shadblow could include pachysandra, myrtle, or ferns and hostas interplanted with early-spring-flowering miniature bulbs.

Shadblow is easy to transplant. To give mass and line to a garden and to introduce white flowers in April, I bought an eight-foot shadblow from a local nursery several years ago. I set it at the back of an eight-foot-deep perennial border, adding generous amounts of well-decomposed cow manure to the moist, loamy soil. The spring transplant took readily and now forms the central focus of the bed. In a narrower bed, I could have planted 'Regent', a compact, denser cultivar of the related *A. alnifolia*.

Shadblow can also be combined at the edge of a woodland with other shrubs such as the royal azalea (*Rhododendron schlippenbachii*). Shadblow's airy growth habit and delicate white

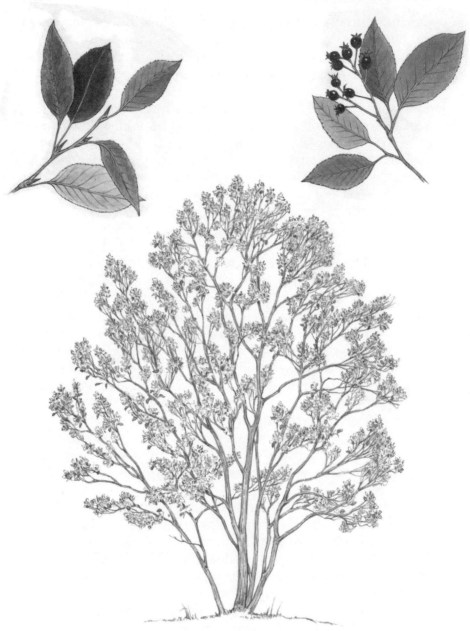

One of the earliest shrubs to bloom in New England, shadblow can be planted within your perennial bed, at the edge of a woodland, or as part of a foundation planting. Its white blossoms, smooth gray bark, and delicate tracery of branches makes it appealing wherever you grow it.

bloom contrast with the more compact habit and larger pink flowers of the azaleas. (The contrast is enhanced with evergreens as a background.) The shrubs can be underplanted with blue grape hyacinths (*Muscari armeniacum*), species tulips such as *Tulipa tarda*, trout lilies (*Erythronium* species), Juliana hybrid primroses, *Pulmonaria officinalis*, *Sanguinaria canadensis*, or *Viola odorata*. A shadblow planted amid any of these plants will usher in spring in an elegant fashion.

7

BEARBERRY

Bearberry is a ground-hugging evergreen shrub that's equally at home in a rock garden in Boulder, Colorado, in an exposed seaside garden outside Camden, Maine, or as a groundcover to hold a sandy bank in Hannibal, Missouri. And it's tough, as its formidable botanical name, *Arctostaphylos uva-ursi*, implies. It flourishes in gravelly, acidic mountainside soil in full sun across its vast native range—from the outer edge of the Arctic Circle (Zone 2), south to Virginia (Zone 7), and west to northern New Mexico and Arizona (Zone 6). It also finds a niche in acidic beach sand, where it forms broad, salt-tolerant, six-inch-high mats.

As an ornamental, bearberry doesn't miss a beat. From one end of the growing season to the other, its quarter-inch oval leaves are dark green and glossy. In early fall the leaves turn reddish-bronze and hold that color into early spring. In late April and May clusters of pink-tinged, white, urn-shaped flowers form. By late July or early August they develop into lustrous scarlet berries that persist well into autumn, attracting birds. The stems of this trailing shrub conform to the shapes of rocks and slopes over which they flow. As the branches mature, they become covered with a papery, reddish exfoliating bark. 'Massachusetts', a recent selection and a good alternative to the species, has denser and darker foliage and is more free-flowering.

Fred Watson, a friend from East Alstead, New Hampshire, used bearberry as part of what he refers to as ground tapestry in his rock garden. Four years ago, he planted a drift of about 25 rooted cuttings 8 to 12 inches apart. Near this he planted a *Juniperus procumbens* 'Nana', whose blue-green moss-like foliage is an attractive contrast to bearberry leaves and fruit. To develop the effect he put in drifts of sempervivums, heathers,

With reddish-bronze foliage in winter and glossy dark-green leaves in summer, bearberry is a hardy trailing shrub for use as a groundcover, as a plant flowing over rocks in the rock garden, or cascading over the tops of retaining walls.

Androsace sarmentosa, and *Draba sibirica.* Now the plants are a carpet of colors and textures that flow up, around, and between gray, lichen-covered rocks, at the same time forming groundcover for such plants as *Rhododendron kiusianum, Pinus sylvestris,* and *Tsuga canadensis* 'Hussii'. In this situation, yearly pruning of the vigorous bearberry is necessary, but ordinarily it doesn't require pruning.

Besides using bearberry in rock gardens, or to secure sunny banks, I've planted it in soil a foot or so behind the tops of stone retaining walls. It has flourished there, flowing back into drought-tolerant shrub beds and down over the side to soften the wall. When planting bearberry in open sandy loam in well-drained soils, I add no amendments. But before planting in heavier topsoil, I dig in hefty amounts of sand or gravel to increase drainage.

If you ask at the nursery for bearberry and no one recognizes the name, you could ask for hog cranberry, mealberry, mountain box, bear's grape, sandberry, creashak, or kinnikinick, for *Arctostaphylos uva-ursi* has many common names.

8

MOUNTAIN LAUREL

There's a town named after laurel in Delaware, Florida, Indiana, Maryland, Mississippi, Montana, Nebraska, New Jersey, Ohio, and Pennsylvania. Winsted, Connecticut, is known as the Laurel City, and celebrates with a festival at the height of the blooming season. Drive through villages in the rural East and ask if there's a Laurel Way or a Laurel Road. More often than not, the answer will be yes.

People like laurel a lot. Ernest Henry Wilson, eminent plant collector and curator of Boston's Arnold Arboretum for years, was no exception. In his book, *If I Were to Plant a Garden*, he wrote, "This is the broad-leaf evergreen par excellence. A clump of restful green for eleven months of the year, then an unmatched wealth of loveliness, a myriad of blossoms artfully fashioned, burst into clouds of white and delicate pink."

You may have noticed that some nurseries have recently introduced new cultivars of mountain laurel. The man behind virtually all of those introductions is Richard Jaynes. In his fifties, Dick Jaynes is a broad-shouldered, easy-going man with graying, crew-cut hair and an angular face.

In 1961, with a degree from Wesleyan University in biology and a doctorate from Yale in botany, Jaynes took a position with the Connecticut Agricultural Experiment Station in New Haven. First as a geneticist and later as a horticulturist, he spent more than 20 years researching and hybridizing within the genus *Kalmia*, the American laurels. But it's only within the last few years that the results of his work have begun to appear in catalogs.

What Jaynes hoped to give nurserymen and the gardening public through his breeding efforts was a greater choice of plants than nature offered. As beautiful as native mountain laurel is, the species has a tendency to grow open and leggy.

Jaynes, like other hybridizers, wanted to create a denser, more compact plant. He also wanted to experiment with the pinkish-white flower to develop more intense pinks and reds. And he wanted to provide Southern nurserymen with a more heat-tolerant mountain laurel.

CROSSING THE SPECIES

Jaynes' first order of business was to determine whether species within this genus belonging to the heath family, Ericaceae, could be crossed to produce hybrids of horticultural interest. There are seven species of *Kalmia* native to North America and Cuba. Jaynes had six species to work with: *K. microphylla,* western alpine laurel; *K. polifolia,* eastern bog laurel; *K. angustifolia,* sheep laurel; *K. cuneata,* white wicky; *K. hirsuta,* sandhill laurel; and *K. latifolia,* the mountain laurel. (Jaynes was unable to obtain the seventh species, *K. ericoides,* native to Cuba.) Theoretically, they formed a rich gene pool, with each species contributing its own leaf form, branching pattern, growth habit, hardiness, soil preference, and flower form and color.

Kalmia latifolia, the familiar mountain laurel, is a shrub that rarely exceeds 12 feet in height. It was clearly the most important species in the hybridizing program because it has attractive flowers and growth habit, three- to five-inch evergreen leaves that don't curl in the winter nearly as much as rhododendrons' do, and is highly versatile. It can be used as a specimen, foundation, or woodland plant.

After much trial and error over 20 years, Jaynes concluded that only one interspecific cross would interest nurserymen, *K. latifolia* × *K. hirsuta. Kalmia hirsuta,* the sandhill laurel (named for the short hairs that grow along its stems), is two feet high with half-inch flowers, and blooms from early summer to autumn, the longest blooming period of any *Kalmia* species. Sandhill laurel is native to the coastal plains of the Southeast from southern Alabama and northern Florida, north through Georgia to the southeast tip of South Carolina. (Jaynes received his original seeds and plants from Tom Dodd, a wholesale nurseryman in Semmes, Alabama.) Its common name derives

Years of breeding have created many appealing cultivars of mountain laurel, an evergreen shrub with flowers ranging from white to cinnamon, pink, and red. Look for the new hybrids and cultivars just coming onto the market.

from its habit of growing in low, sandy pine savannas, sand-hills, and dunes. Jaynes and Dodd were also interested in *Kalmia hirsuta*'s preference for dry conditions.

Jaynes has several specimens of *K. latifolia* × *K. hirsuta* in his trial beds in Hamden, Connecticut. The hybrid has a dense, bushy growth habit much like that of evergreen azaleas, yet the flowers resemble the standard mountain laurel's. The leaves are leathery and lance-shaped, about an inch long. Small hairs cover the stems, particularly near the tips of new growth.

Tom Dodd and his son heard of the successful cross and expressed an interest early on. Jaynes sent them seeds and cuttings in the mid 1970s. Tom Dodd, Jr., wrote that the un-named *K. latifolia* × *K. hirsuta* hybrid would "be hardy in Zones 7, 8, and 9, and possibly 6 [the zone Jaynes works in]. The hybrid is quite heat-tolerant and blooms most of the summer here in Alabama."

EXCITING NEW COLORING

Given the limited success of the interspecific breeding pro-gram, Jaynes turned his attention to hybridizing within the richly varied mountain laurel species itself. Like many plants, *K. latifolia* embraces a variety of forms within a single species—25 by one count. Jaynes could have set out to cross all 25 with each other, creating possibly hundreds of F_1 hybrids. (F_1, or first filial, represents the first generation of hybrids that come from uncultivated parents. Crosses between F_1s yield F_2s, and so on.)

Rather than embark on another broad breeding program, Jaynes chose to focus on three forms that he felt might yield hybrids of horticultural interest. First was *K. latifolia* 'Fuscata', or banded mountain laurel. Its flowers have a brownish-purple to cinnamon band within the cup-shaped corolla. Some speci-mens have broader bands than others, some are interrupted, and still others have bands so broad that they almost fill the corolla. Here was a laurel that promised exciting new coloring.

The second form Jaynes selected was *K. latifolia* 'Myrtifolia', a miniature with myrtle-like leaves. It has all the beauty and charm of the familiar mountain laurel save its stature. Rare in

the wild, it had the potential to spawn an intermediate cultivar—a laurel with a more compact habit of growth (a plant
anyone familiar with leggy, older specimens of K. *latifolia* could
appreciate).

The third group of plants he entered into his intraspecific
hybridizing plans were those that had distinctly red or pink
flowers. He was hoping to develop new cultivars that would
combine small stature or compact growth habit with banded
coloring in the corolla and deeper pinks and reds in the flower
bud.

This breeding program brought more satisfying results. By
1980 the Connecticut Agricultural Experiment Station had an-
nounced seven new hybrids of mountain laurel and made them
available to the nursery trade. These extended the range of
flower form and color, foliage form, and shrub habit available
in mountain laurels (see chart). 'Goodrich', 'Nipmuck', 'Pink
Charm', 'Pink Surprise', 'Quinnipiac', 'Shooting Star', and
'Stillwood' are on the retail market now. The precise hardiness
range of these hybrids has not yet been determined with certainty, but some are as hardy as the parent plants and should
thrive in Zones 4 and 5. Others, like the red-budded laurels,
may do best in protected areas in Zone 5 or farther south.

In November 1983, Jaynes formally introduced to the scientific community five more hybrids, perhaps the most dramatic
in terms of color: 'Elf', 'Bullseye', 'Sarah', 'Freckles', and 'Car-
ousel'.

'SHOOTING STAR'

After 25 years at the experiment station, Jaynes resigned in
April 1984, when the state of Connecticut phased out the laurel
project. Today he is continuing his work on *Kalmia* at his own
Broken Arrow Nursery in Hamden. He has successfully
crossed the miniature 'Myrtifolia' form with K. *latifolia* 'An-
gustata', willow-leaved mountain laurel, creating a miniature
with especially attractive foliage and flowers. It will be most
satisfactory in small backyard or rock gardens. Through further
work with this cross (which is not yet available to home gardeners), Jaynes hopes to create a range of miniature mountain

NEW CULTIVARS OF

Cultivar	Bud Color	Open Flower
'Bullseye'	Off-white	Broad, purplish-cinnamon band on inside of flower with white center and edge
'Carousel'	Off-white	Intricate banding of bright purplish-cinnamon within flower cup
'Elf'	Light pink	Nearly white
'Freckles'	Light pink	10 purplish-cinnamon "freckles" circle inside of flower just above each anther pocket
'Goodrich'	Off-white	Cinnamon-brown band broken with white between anther filaments; rimmed in white
'Nipmuck' (Similar to 'Quinnipiac' but with lighter-green foliage)	Intense red	White at first, turning to pink
'Ostbo Red'	Iridescent red	White at first, turning pink
'Pink Surprise'	Deep pink	Pink
'Sarah'	Brilliant red	Pink-red
'Shooting Star'	Light pink, almost white	White to light pink
'Silver Dollar'	Light pink	White with pink blush; rose-colored ring at base and rosy spots near anther pockets

*USDA Hardiness Zones given here are estimates. The cold-tolerance of these new cultivars has not been established.

MOUNTAIN LAUREL

Foliage and Habit	Hardiness*	Comments
Like species: dark green, oblong leaves, fairly compact habit but tends to grow open and leggy; at maturity 8'–12' high	Zone 5	Banded, or 'Fuscata', form
Like species	Zone 5	Banded
Compact; one-third to one-half the size of standard laurel	Zone 5	Unusual and rare miniature form; flowers are like species, but large in proportion to this otherwise compact plant
Tendency to be open and leggy	Zone 5	
Habit a little more open than species	Zone 5	
Yellow-green leaves	Zone 6	Less hardy than other cultivars; in Dick Jaynes' trial beds in Conn., 'Nipmuck' suffered tip dieback during severe winters
Leaves slightly smaller than species; foliage more dense	Zone 6	Flower color most intense when grown in full sun (true of all red-budded mountain laurels); not as cold-tolerant as species
Dark green; full	Zone 5	Responds well to pruning to encourage dense growth; vigorous
Like species	Zone 5	Flowers especially eye-catching
Tends toward leggy, open growth	Zone 6	Unusual flower form with 5 reflexed petals, unlike common cup-shaped corolla; blooms about a week later than species; a bit less hardy than other cultivars
Large, dark, glossy leaves	Zone 5	Exceptionally large flowers; at 1½" across, about twice the size of species

laurel plants with flower traits now available in larger cultivars. He also hopes to produce a solid red flower and a ruffled or double flower.

A significant facet of Jaynes' work has been in selecting notable forms from the wild and from other hybridizers. One such success was recorded in 1971 with *K. latifolia* 'Polypetala', the feather-petaled form of mountain laurel. His colleague Hollis Rogers sent Jaynes slides of 'Polypetala' that he had photographed near Danbury, North Carolina. The slide showed a laurel flower like none other Jaynes had seen. Its white to light-pink corolla was deeply cut. It looked much like the flowers of shooting-star (*Dodecatheon* species).

"The minute I looked at the slides," Jaynes said, "I knew Hollis had found a unique and exciting new plant. A few days later we received flowers, pollen, and cuttings from him and began to make crosses and grafts." It has since been introduced to the retail market under the name 'Shooting Star'. With a delicate flower and reflexed petals, it blooms one to two weeks later than most other mountain laurels.

Edmund Mezitt of Weston Nurseries in Hopkinton, Massachusetts, has also been selecting and hybridizing plants from the wild, on his own and in cooperation with Jaynes. Through him, Weston introduced the mountain laurel selection 'Silver Dollar', named for its dramatic flowers the size of the coins.

PLANTING YOUR OWN

If you've admired mountain laurel and would like to plant it in your own garden, there are two fundamental matters you need to consider. All need acidic soil, and some need special attention to siting. In the right light and soil, mountain laurel is a beautiful, trouble-free plant. Provided with shelter from severe wind and reflected sunlight, it tolerates full sun. In fact, the more sun mountain laurel receives (up to a point), the more dense will be its growth and the more prolific its flowering.

Because mountain laurel, like other broad-leaved evergreens, continues to transpire (give off water from its leaves) throughout the winter, it cannot thrive where exposed to drying winds and intense sunlight reflected off buildings. When using mountain laurel as a foundation plant, set it out on the east or north side of the house. There the plant is shaded, daytime temperatures are moderated, and leaves do not lose as much moisture as they would on the more exposed sides.

Southern and western exposures can be tempered by setting laurel several feet away from the house or by setting it under deciduous trees. Jaynes warns that siting becomes increasingly important in the middle to southern part of laurel's useful range, where sun in summer is more intense.

Most *Kalmia* species are found in nature in soils with a pH of 4.5 to 5.5. Without acidic soil, mountain laurel cannot take up iron in sufficient amounts, and iron chlorosis can set in. If your soil tests out above 5.5, lower the pH by adding aluminum sulfate, ferrous sulfate, or sulfur. The first two compounds work quickly, changing the pH within two or three weeks. Sulfur, much less expensive and longer-lasting, will take between six and nine weeks.

Be especially careful about pH level if you are planting laurels near foundations. The soil there is typically more alkaline because of construction debris like sheetrock, plaster, and cement. Calcium leached from masonry walls will also raise the pH over the years.

Mountain laurel also requires well-drained, highly organic soil. When you've chosen an appropriate site for your plant, dig a hole twice the size of its root ball. Separate the topsoil from the subsoil as you dig, and discard subsoil. Throw the topsoil back into the hole and then add an equal amount of wetted peat moss and as much compost and leaf mold as you can. (Of trees common to backyards, oaks have the most acidic leaves.) Mix the peat, compost, leaf mold, and topsoil well, and then plant the mountain laurel. If your soil is heavy with clay, add generous amounts of coarse sand along with the peat moss and leaf mold. Water well at planting time and during dry spells.

Having planted and watered the shrub, mulch it with two to three inches of wood chips, pine bark, or needles. Maintain that level of mulch over the years. As Jaynes notes, "None of the laurels will thrive in an exposed location where the soil is left bare and the ground freezes deep in the winter or dries out in the summer."

In the fall, pull back the mulch, water thoroughly, and re-place the mulch, so that the young shrub will go into the winter with adequate moisture. In subsequent years loosen the soil under the plant before replenishing mulch and sprinkle cotton-seed meal (7-2-2) on the ground, following instructions on the bag. This fertilizer will provide nutrients during the spring growth surge and will also increase soil acidity.

Early spring, before buds break, is the best time to set out new transplants. Purchase your plants rather than dig them from the wild.

Before buying any mountain laurel or any other *Kalmia* spe-cies or hybrids now coming onto the market, be certain that plants you buy are hardy for your area. "Species like mountain laurel with an extensive north-south range may vary greatly in their hardiness," Jaynes cautions. "Plants from the southern end of the range are not suited to the north, with its shorter, colder growing season, and will not adapt to it." For this reason it's best to purchase plants that have been grown in your region. Always ask your nurseryman where his plants were grown. Consider the hardiness zone of the nursery from which you order plants.

CARING FOR LAURELS

If some of the leaves of newly transplanted laurels are browned after their first winter, pick them off in early spring. Wait until summer to make certain twigs or branches are dead before pruning them back to healthy new shoots.

Mountain laurel and other *Kalmia* respond well to heavy pruning, but they rarely require it if planted properly. The best way to get (and keep) a shrub in good shape is to prune it every year. Prune back a few limbs to forks, not limb ends, or to small laterals so that the plant can fill out. This pruning can be done at any time of the year. Jaynes adds that there is a drastic but nonetheless effective method of regenerating neglected laurels: Cut the limbs off two or three inches above the ground in early spring. In three to four years you will have a new, bushy plant. (Nurserymen, he notes, have used this method for years when collecting plants from the wild.) Cut off spent flower heads at their bases immediately after they die to encourage a rich annual bloom.

Once established, laurels are remarkably pest- and disease-resistant. The most serious and commonly seen disease of mountain laurel is chlorosis, or yellowing of leaves; the veins remain green. It typically attacks the plant when the soil pH is above 5.5, but it can also be caused by soil compaction or black vine weevil, which sometimes attacks the roots. According to Jaynes, it can also result from improper fertilizing, winter injury to roots, or too much nitrogen.

He encourages gardeners to determine if any of the problems noted above other than high pH could be the cause. If soil tests show that the pH is too high, chlorosis can often be immediately reversed by applying chelated iron, either as a drench or foliar spray, and by adding ferrous sulfate to lower the pH.

To eradicate brown fungus spots that form on the leaves, spray twice with an all-purpose fungicide, first when new leaves are half developed and later when they are fully developed. An all-purpose insecticide will adequately deal with the few insects that attack laurel.

Lovely as they are, *Kalmia* species share to varying degrees a poison in their leaves. Andromedotoxin, which is toxic to animals, is present in all *Kalmia* leaves. If you raise cattle, goats, or sheep, don't let them graze in fields where mountain, sheep, or western alpine laurel grows unless you're sure there's other graze in the fields. Animals will only graze on *Kalmia* if there's nothing else to eat.

Above all, mountain laurel is beautiful the year round—in spring with its delicate bloom, and in summer, fall, and winter with its handsome growth habit and evergreen foliage. Give it what it needs and you'll enjoy the plant for decades with very little work.

Laurels are equally attractive as specimen plants or in clumps. Furthermore, the colors of the newly introduced hybrids are all complementary. Reds, pinks, whites, and cinnamon-reds can be placed next to one another. Jaynes suggests grouping them in threes. You can put a white between a pink and a red, or a red between two whites—say, 'Silver Dollar' framed by 'Pink Frost' and 'Ostbo Red'. How many and what kinds of new mountain laurel introductions will appear in the next 20 years is anyone's guess, but one thing is certain— virtually all of them will be descendants of plants Jaynes hybridized.

9

CLIMBING HYDRANGEA

The climbing hydrangea (*Hydrangea anomala* subsp. *petiolaris*) can scramble up the trunk of an 80-foot tree and, there in the shade, throw hundreds upon hundreds of white flowers in June. On the ground, its heart-shaped leaves can cover any large, shady bank or rock pile. It can also grow on a trellis or on the shady face of a brick, stone, or concrete wall, and here in the Northeast it will cover any such site with a cascade of glossy, dark-green leaves from May to September. Let it grow up the side of a wooden barn, and throughout the winter its golden stems will form a handsome tracery to catch the snow. After the outset of its third year it requires no training or tying; it seems to know exactly where to go and clings with root-like holdfasts.

Considering its many merits, climbing hydrangea can be surprisingly hard to find at the average garden center. Six years ago my wife and I had difficulty locating a transplant, even in the mailorder catalogs. Since then I've discovered many catalogs that list the plant. Perhaps Americans haven't bought climbing hydrangea more often because it doesn't look particularly promising in the nursery. The transplant we eventually found was a 12-inch stick with a few meager side shoots, which happens to be just the size and sort of plant most appropriate for setting out. Well-established plants are difficult to move. Climbing hydrangea has the deserved reputation of being a slow starter that exacts its measure of patience from the most forgiving of gardeners. Given time, though, the unprepossessing young plants turn into extraordinarily vigorous and dramatic vines.

We set out our plant in spring, in compost-enriched topsoil, about a foot from our garden shed. For the first season nothing changed about the 12-inch stick except that it sprouted a few leaves. The second year the leader advanced a couple of inches, and several side shoots did likewise, but that was about it. With the onset of the third season it truly took hold, lending credence to the old Vermont saying about transplants: "The first year it sleeps, the second year it creeps, the third year it leaps." That year the four main stems grew at least three feet, and each gave rise to 18-inch-long lateral stems.

At the end of its fourth year, our climbing hydrangea covered an area seven feet high and four feet wide. And it bloomed for the first time—10 or 15 flower heads holding for two weeks. They turned an attractive buff-brown as they dried, and they lasted well into the fall when we snipped several off for small dried-flower arrangements. The dull-green autumn foliage was of little interest.

Once the leaves dropped, the cinnamon-brown bark of the main trunk, by then five-year-old wood, began to shred and peel away in an attractive fashion. Furthermore, one- and two-year-old shoots remained a luminous yellow-brown throughout the winter, bringing light and color to the shady, northern wall of the shed. These young side shoots, up to three feet tall and growing on either side of the main stems, now overlap one another to form the network of bright shoots against the barn boards.

A VERSATILE VINE

The English have known about this Asian native for decades. At Sissinghurst Castle, in Kent, Vita Sackville-West planted it on a brick wall framing the entrance leading to the Rose Garden from the formal Tower Lawn. The vines form a cascade of foliage 10 feet high and 20 or 30 feet wide. At Hidcote Manor, Lawrence Johnston trained the vine up a north-facing wall of Cotswold stone. Planted several decades ago, it now forms billows of lustrous foliage behind a group of ferns near a stone sculpture.

In various other English gardens, I've seen climbing hydrangea combined with such shade-loving or shade-tolerant species as azaleas, rhododendrons, skimmia, leucothoe, box, mahonia, fatsia, and pieris, to name a few shrubs that thrive under similar conditions. In her book, *Color in Your Garden,*

Penelope Hobhouse notes how the dark-green foliage of *Hydrangea petiolaris* can be used to cool hotter colors such as the bright orange of tulips. She writes elsewhere that you can interplant it with variegated ivy, a contrast that tends to lighten the dark leaves of the hydrangea (as its own flowers do).

I've also seen the vine trained up to and along the top of an eight-foot-high brick wall. In this case the lower side shoots had been pruned off to enable the gardener to use the wall, rather than the vine, as a backdrop for shrubs and perennials. There are many perennials for shade that would work well in such a setting, whether the lower stems of the hydrangea are cut off or not. In the back of the border you could put *Cimicifuga racemosa*, rodgersias, and thalictrums; in the middle, foxglove, bleeding heart, various ferns, and the taller hostas; in the front, epimediums, hardy geraniums, candelabra primroses, spiderworts, and bergenias.

Alan Haskell, a rare-plant collector and landscape gardener from New Bedford, Massachusetts, is one American who knows climbing hydrangea well. He told me of a vine he planted several years ago at the base of a Chinese elm. Last June the vine threw some 500 flower heads from the top to the bottom of the 40-foot tree, which shades the hydrangea. The vine does no harm to the tree.

In Harold Epstein's garden in Larchmont, New York, I saw several 40-year-old vines growing up 100-year-old black and red oaks. Epstein says that while driving in the mountains of Hokkaido, in northern Japan, one late July, he had the impression there was a snowstorm within a deciduous forest. Approaching it, he realized he was actually seeing thousands of mature climbing hydrangeas in full bloom.

WHERE TO PLANT

If you're considering planting climbing hydrangea, be sure not to set it against a wall that requires frequent maintenance. And certainly don't plant it against a clapboard wall. It will creep underneath the boards and pull them loose. Any mature hardwood tree (with the exception of the maple, whose thick surface roots would present too much competition), or an open softwood tree such as white pine, would make a good support

A handsome and vigorous flowering vine, climbing hydrangea will add year-round interest to your garden, whether growing 60 feet up into an oak tree, covering a north-facing stone, brick, or concrete wall, or gracing a brick or stone chimney.

for this vine. Try using it to cover a north- or east-facing outcrop of rock or ledge, if you have one. Use it to cover an arbor or patio structure in the shade, on a trellis to form a summer screen against work areas, or simply to enclose sections of your garden. The climbing hydrangea is a good vine for coastal gardens too. It's drought-resistant, able to withstand the rigors of wind, and virtually free of pests and diseases.

I've found climbing hydrangea simple to propagate by layering in spring, once the plant is at least four years old. In fact, the vine seems to do this by itself, especially when used as a groundcover. I place a small, flat stone atop several lower stems to hold them firmly against the soil and encourage rooting. The following spring I snip those rooted stems off at the trunk and plant them.

Once established, climbing hydrangea gives new meaning to the word "vigorous." Nowhere have I seen a better example of this trait than at the Case Estates, in Weston, Massachusetts (an annex of the Arnold Arboretum). There you'll find a display of 157 different groundcovers, all lined up in neat rows of adjacent four-by-four-foot plots. The other 156 remain within their confines, but the climbing hydrangea creeps and clambers and climbs up the stone wall behind its allotted space, along the top of the wall, and, when I saw it, up and over a trellis beyond.

You can prune it in late fall or early spring, but to show climbing hydrangea to its best advantage, let it go.

10 🌸

SWEET PEPPERBUSH

One mid-August afternoon several years ago, my wife and I were visiting friends who had recently bought a summer home on a lake in southern New Hampshire. We were lazing on the dock enjoying the clear, crisp air when a breeze carried a fragrance to us that I recognized as coming from the sweet pepperbush (*Clethra alnifolia*), so named for its peppercorn-like fruit capsules. We put on our shoes and walked into the undergrowth at the edge of the lake and there, hidden from view by saplings, were hundreds of two- to three-foot-high sweet pepperbushes, all in full bloom. The spicy, sweet fragrance of the creamy-white blossoms filled the woodland. The next spring we bought three *Clethra* for our garden from a local nursery.

In early August, when most other shrubs have completed their flowering, sweet pepperbush comes into full bloom, and the florets can last for most of the month. Granted, hypericums, hydrangeas, orange-eye buddleias, potentillas, and a very few other shrubs are in bloom then. But not one of them combines so many attributes: sweetly scented flowers; finely proportioned, dark green foliage that turns yellow or orange in the autumn; an oval and unfettered growth habit, the upright lines of which are pleasing throughout the winter; and an unusually broad hardiness range. (It flourishes in nature from southern Maine to Florida and west to eastern Texas.)

Summersweet, another of its common names, can be used in many places in the garden. It will tolerate relatively dry sites, but it does best in naturally moist, rich, acidic soil. It can be planted as a single specimen plant or naturalized at the edge of a pond or lake. It makes a fine addition to a shrub border with other moisture-tolerant plants such *Enkianthus campanulatus*, *Lindera benzoin*, *Ilex glabra*, *Chamaecyparis pisifera*, *Rhododendron vaseyi*, and some viburnums. It works well in a seaside garden.

No other shrub that blooms at the unusual time of August has such clean lines, fragrant blossoms, and finely proportioned foliage as the sweet pepperbush. And in late winter, watch chickadees jounce the twigs to loosen peppercorn-like seed capsules onto the snow.

On Block Island, Rhode Island, for example, it grows so widely that local beekeepers are able to make and sell clethra honey.

The sweet pepperbush can also be planted under the eaves of a house where, even if the limbs are snapped by the weight of falling snow, the shrub will still bloom because its five-inch flower spikes arise from the tips of new wood. Plant it next to a door on either of the eave sides of the house—the roof will shed the extra water the sweet pepperbush prefers—and in August its fragrance will waft into the house. To call attention to it in spring, when it may appear lifeless, underplant it with maidenhair ferns, in turn interplanted with miniature spring-blooming bulbs and Virginia bluebells.

Clethra alnifolia and its three cultivars are available through many nurseries and mailorder houses. 'Rosea' has glossier foliage than the species and throws light pink flower buds. When open, the flowers are initially pink but gradually turn white. 'Pink Spires' also carries pink buds, a color the flowers retain. 'Paniculata', introduced as early as 1770, has considerably greater vigor than the parent, with larger flowers and slightly arching branches.

The species and its cultivars have a reputation for being slow to establish. So when planting sweet pepperbush pay close attention to site and soil preparation. Choose a spot with naturally occurring moisture in sun or light shade in soil with a pH between 4 and 6. Dig a hole at least three times the size of the rootball and add lots of compost and peat. Plant the container-grown or balled and burlapped shrub only in the early spring. Water, and mulch with at least four inches of white pine needles or chipped bark. And don't be alarmed if the shrub you purchase looks lifeless in the early spring—the sweet pepperbush is among the latest to leaf out.

Once it becomes established, after two or three years, your sweet pepperbush will flourish for decades, remaining free of pests and diseases. However, if the soil dries, the stressed plant will be susceptible to red spider mites. Over the years, transplants spread slowly by means of underground shoots that form around the central crown of the plant. Depending on soil, moisture, and climate, it will mature to a dense and leafy shrub with a height of four to eight feet and a width of four to six feet.

The sweet pepperbush doesn't need regular pruning, but an overlarge or crowded plant can be cut back in early winter. (Early-spring pruning can cause bleeding.) Prune out the older wood, which is about the diameter of your thumb and blackish, unlike the brownish younger wood.

Propagation is simple. Three- to four-inch lateral cuttings, preferably with a heel of older wood, taken in late summer root readily in sand and peat. Rooted offshoots can be cut from the base of the plant in the fall and planted in a sand-humus mix. In early spring, you can also direct-sow seeds.

Our three plants not only provide us with year-round interest, but also, when their cool fragrance fills one corner of the garden in August, carry us back to that New Hampshire lakeside, linking us with friends and the wide area to which this plant is native.

11

CHOOSING APPLE TREES

I grew up on a fruit farm in Connecticut, but I've been off the farm now for 20 years. And when it came time one winter for my wife and me to choose a few apple trees for our backyard, I was overwhelmed by all the new varieties, not to mention the paragraphs and diagrams explaining interstems and clonal understock.

Luckily, we visited my family recently on the farm that my father started in the early 1930s, and I broached the subject with him and my brother Peter, who took over the farm a few years back. "How do we select two or three apple trees out of this myriad of information?" I asked as I held up several catalogs. Peter immediately went to his files and returned with what he regards as *the* fruit tree catalog. It was from Hilltop Orchards and Nurseries, Route 2, Hartford, Michigan 49057. It contained virtually everything I needed to know to select fruit stock: the older varieties; the newer ones; planting instructions; information on pruning, pollination, and thinning. It was well laid out and clearly written.

In addition, he gave me the names of three other nurseries that he regards highly: Adams County Nursery, Aspers, Pennsylvania 17034; Stark Brothers Nursery, Louisiana, Missouri 63353; New York State Fruit Testing Cooperative Association, Geneva, New York 14456.

As to selecting specific trees, my father said I had to consider a few things before making that decision. The major consideration concerns cross-pollination characteristics of each variety. All apple trees, to one degree or another, require pollination across varieties. 'Red Delicious', for example, is a popular apple tree, but it doesn't pollinate easily. 'Rhode Island Greenings' are a poor source of pollen and would require at least two other varieties nearby for all three to cross-pollinate. My wife and I would have to choose two or three trees that would be compatible regarding pollination.

Another consideration, my brother said, was whether we wanted summer or winter apples. If we ordered only the former, in four or five years we would get bushels of apples all at once sometime in August. But they wouldn't keep for more than three or four weeks. Of the old standards, he recommended 'Early Macs' or the 'Wealthy' variety. For a cooking apple, he suggested 'R.I. Greenings'. Of the more recently developed varieties, he suggested 'Jerseymac', 'Paula-red', or 'Tydeman's Red'.

He went on to say that if we wanted winter apples—that is, storing apples, which would mature in late September or October—he recommended 'Empire', 'Macoun', and 'Idared' as good newer varieties. Of the older ones, 'Cortland' and 'McIntosh' headed his list.

If you live in the planting zone that stretches from Virginia to Texas, you might consider 'York', 'Rome', or 'Granny Smith' varieties. If you live in the warmest climates of the country, consider 'Anna', 'Tropical Beauty', 'Elin Shemer', and 'Orleans' varieties.

You might find disease-resistant types—'Prima', 'Priscilla', and 'Liberty'—featured in your catalogs. These indeed fend off fungal diseases, but they won't hold off insects any better than the other varieties. If you want relatively clean fruit even on the disease-resistant trees, you'll probably have to apply an insecticide every two weeks from mid April to early August. Given that there are so few disease-resistant varieties anyway, you may as well expand your choices and consider the whole spectrum of varieties and then apply an all-purpose fruit tree spray every two weeks. Of course, if you object to chemical sprays, then the disease-resistant varieties are clearly for you.

There is one other important consideration: tree size—dwarf, semidwarf, or standard? Virtually all varieties are available in all three sizes. My wife and I finally chose the semidwarfs, which mature at from eight to ten feet in height. We stayed away from dwarf trees, which range from three to seven feet in height at maturity, because many of them were developed for intensive commercial plantings. Certain rootstocks to which dwarf variety scions are grafted don't anchor well, and thus the tree requires staking. On the other hand, the standard-size trees mature at 25 feet or more, an unmanageable height requiring costly equipment.

The semidwarf trees sounded the best and will give us some fruit within two years after planting. But here is a word of caution: Watch the wording in the catalogs. *Dwarf* in one might mean *semidwarf* in another. Look for the tree that matures at a height that you and the ladder out in the garage can handle.

If you've decided to plant apple trees, send for the catalogs this fall and place your order, but be ready to wait up to a year and a half to receive the really fine trees from the best nurseries. The trees might cost anywhere from $10 to $15 each, but they'll be worth it.

BULBS, PERENNIALS, and WILDFLOWERS

The next step in creating a garden is to decide which bulbs, perennials, and wildflowers you'll plant, and where. It's easy to be overwhelmed by the many choices in the glossy catalogs, and so it's hard to know where to start. A good way to get organized is to have a blank sheet of paper for each of the months in your gardening season. Then choose a favorite larger flowering perennial for each month. For example, one of my choices might be bee balm. It blooms in late June and throughout July in Vermont, so I assign it to the July sheet. Then I ask, what would go well with its red blooms and two- to three-foot height? (This is when you would look in the catalogs or your own garden for answers.) Last season, I combined bee balm with Coreopsis verticillata 'Moonbeam', with its pale yellow, long-lasting blooms, and Nepeta faassenii 'Six Hills Giant' for its lavender blooms and low mounding habit. Once that threesome was established, I selected other plants that would complement that combination for an attractive garden picture in July.

The following chapters are more extensive examples of this same process, and they should give you the confidence to create your own satisfying shrub-perennial-bulb combinations.

12 🌼

EARLY-SPRING BULBS

It was in the southern New Hampshire garden of my good friend Howard Andros that I learned how early-spring bulbs can be brought into "the garden proper," as Gertrude Jekyll calls it, by combining them with ferns. I was pruning trees next door to his house one mid-April morning when Howard, a white-haired gentleman who had spent the better part of his life as a professional plantsman, walked over and invited me for a cup of soup. On our way to the house, we walked into his yard to see the late show of snowdrops and snowflakes and the early crocuses and aconites under a lilac hedge not yet in leaf.

Twenty years ago, to form a backdrop for an eight-foot-deep perennial bed, Howard had planted a 50-foot-long hedge of French hybrid lilacs. They don't sucker like *Syringa vulgaris* and are thus more manageable. He's kept this hedge 10 to 12 feet high by cutting back the 15 or so largest trunks in the hedge each year after bloom.

Over the intervening years, he set free-form drifts of five to seven maidenhair ferns (*Adiantum pedatum*), evergreen Christmas ferns (*Polystichum acrostichoides*), and royal ferns (*Osmunda regalis*) in the organically rich and moist soil among the trunks as well as two to three feet out from them, leaving a foot or two between each pair of drifts for the bulbs.

When he found time and energy each fall, he set 50 or more bulbs of either the common snowdrop (*Galanthus nivalis*), with its pendulous white and green flowers; bright-yellow winter aconites (*Eranthus hyemalis*); large-flowering Dutch crocus (*Crocus vernus*) in yellows, whites, purples, and blues; and the green-and-white spring snowflake (*Leucojum vernum*) between those drifts. (Grape hyacinths were noticeably absent because Howard regards them as aggressive self-seeders.) Because the

Crocuses, winter aconites, and snowdrops interplanted with royal or maidenhair ferns growing under lilacs creates a pleasing succession of colors and textures in spring. As the ripening leaves of the miniature bulbs turn yellow, they'll be hidden by the unfurling fronds of the ferns that later form the backdrop for perennials.

colors of early-spring bulbs are so compatible, Howard successfully juxtaposed them in any number of ways.

With each spring now, there is a satisfying progression of
color among Howard's lilacs: snowflakes and snowdrops in
late March and April, followed by aconites and crocuses. Then,
as the foliage from early bulbs begins to die back in late April,
the ferns unfurl: the dark-red stems of the maidenhair with
their light-green foliage, the yellow-green fronds of the royal
fern, and the bright new fronds of the Christmas fern rising
from the darker green fronds still flattened from the recently
melted snow. This array of textures and colors from the ferns
serves to hide the yellowing and unattractive foliage of the
bulbs. By late spring, once they have filled out, the ferns form a
handsome background for such perennials as candelabra primulas, globeflowers, white dicentra, and red and white baneberry that lasts until frost. And because the ferns are not
invasive, Howard has easily been able to maintain a good
balance over the years between the number of ferns and the
more diminutive but spreading bulbs.

After admiring the early-spring bulbs by the lilac hedge, we
walked up the lawn and stopped just by the southeast corner of
the house near the kitchen door. There Howard uses the same
combination of ferns and bulbs but has added Virginia bluebells (*Mertensia virginica*) for more height and another blue.
This combination forms the understory to five- to six-foot-high
sweet pepperbushes (*Clethra alnifolia*), which in turn are under-
plants for high-pruned (15- to 20-foot) lilacs. The rich interplay
of texture, color, and fragrance extends over the full growing
season: snowflakes, snowdrops, crocuses, bluebells, ferns, lilacs, and then, in August, the fragrance of the sweet pepperbush. It's a combination that takes full advantage of the differ-
ing life cycles and blooming periods of the plants, creating a
more satisfying garden.

13

BLOODROOT

In 1916, Guido von Webern bought a seven-acre tract of un-spoiled land at the corner of North Main Street and Turner Road, about four miles from the center of Dayton, Ohio. He bought the land with the intention of building a house on it. Being a keen horticulturist, he also hoped he might find some interesting native plants. He was not disappointed.

While surveying the property one day in early spring, von Webern happened upon what he recognized as a rare mutation of *Sanguinaria canadensis*, the bloodroot. He knew that the flower of the common bloodroot has 8 to 12 white petals radiating horizontally from a yellow center. But on the flowers he was looking at, even the stamens and carpels were transformed into petals, making the flowers look like miniature white water-lilies.

The common form of the flower he found that day is by far the more familiar of the two. This rhizomatous wild flower grows over the eastern half of North America, from Florida to Alabama, and north to Quebec and Manitoba. Colonies grow in open woodlands or along semishaded roadsides and meadow borders. Bloodroot is also widely cultivated in flower gardens, where its short-lived but beautifully delicate bloom accompanies the main show of daffodils.

During the first week or two of April in southern Vermont, the one to five buds that grow along the upper half of the rhizome begin to swell. Rising from each bud is the nascent leaf, wrapped tightly around the minute flower. The leaf acts as a protective covering for the fragile flower bud. Once the soil is sufficiently warm, the flower and leaf buds, wrapped together but atop their respective scapes and petioles, move up through two to three inches of soil to the surface.

When the leaf is half an inch above the debris of the forest floor and is exposed to the warming sun, it unfurls, and within as short a time as 24 hours the flower blooms. Look closely at

Bloodroot, combined with myrtle, maidenhair fern, and anemone, can make an elegant garden picture when planted beneath pieris, yews, or rhododendrons along the shady side of your house.

the bloom that first day or two and you'll see a distinct lavender hue on the undersides of the petals.

In the next few days, the flower will reach its mature height of three to six inches. The pistils have been mature from the moment the flower opened; the stamens mature as the scape grows. During sunny, warm weather the petals lie horizontal, but with the approach of night or inclement weather the petal tips move upward and in 10 minutes can enclose the delicate reproductive organs in a protective canopy.

Although the flower matures quickly, the deeply lobed leaf grows slowly on its short petiole, forming a sturdy, bluish green backdrop for the flower. At night or during cold and cloudy weather, the fig-shaped leaf can embrace the scape of the flower to afford some protection. With the return of warm, sunny weather, the leaf unfurls again.

Once the flower petals fall—and they do so with one gust of wind—the leaf begins to grow to its mature size, which can be up to a foot across, atop a petiole that is 6 to 12 inches high. It's an attractive leaf that adds to the foliage display of any semi-shade-loving garden. In southern Vermont, the leaf reaches full size by the end of May.

As the leaf matures, so do the seeds. By late April, a one-inch-long seed capsule that looks something like a small pea pod begins to form atop the scape, ripening by mid to late June. If it matures during a warm and dry period, the pod may burst open with such force that the glossy, chestnut-brown seeds are flung 10 feet. On a still day, you can hear the snap.

With the seeds sown and the leaf fully grown, the process of storing nutrients in the rhizome beings. Feeder rootlets, which spring from the lower half of the three-quarter-inch-thick rhizome, gather nutrients from the soil while the leaf does its part. Then, around late July, the leaf begins to brown, gradually yellowing during August. By the first of September nothing remains above ground but the dead and withered leaf.

THREE OPTIONS FOR CULTIVATING

The name bloodroot comes from the acrid, reddish sap of the plant. If you break the rhizome or one of the veins of the leaf, a striking red sap oozes from the wound. In its more southern habitats, bloodroot is known as red puccoon, a word derived from the Indian name for the plant. Another, Indian paint, signifies the plant's importance as a dye. Early settlers in America noted that Indians used bloodroot rhizomes to paint their faces and dye their clothing and basketry. In Quebec, the plant is named *sang dragon*.

Bloodroot was officially registered in the *Pharmacopoeia of the United States* from 1820 to 1913 as a stimulating expectorant and emetic. A salve made from the rhizomes was even tried as a cure for cancer by doctors at Middlesex Hospital in London until it was proved ineffective.

Gardeners who would cultivate this member of the poppy family have three options. The first is to find friends or neighbors who have bloodroot plants growing on their properties. Mark the patches clearly in the spring or summer, when the leaves are prominent. By early or mid September, after the last leaf has died back, dig up the rhizomes with a spading fork. They'll be no more than three inches below the surface. Break off the old and decayed parts.

Don't wait too long to dig up the rhizomes. Around early October in these parts, the plants begin to send out new feeder rootlets that will establish the plant for the next spring. If you dig up the rhizomes after that process has begun, the transplants will take longer to acclimate themselves. If you must put off transplanting for a few days, place the rhizomes in peat moss. Don't water the moss; straight from the bale it contains enough moisture to keep the rhizomes from drying out.

Bloodroot rhizomes transplant easily and successfully. Though the plants thrive in the semishade of light filtered through deciduous trees, they will accept full sun if given only moderate amounts of moisture. It's best not to plant the rhizomes under maple trees, as the delicate feeder rootlets cannot compete with the shallow roots of the maple.

Bloodroot flourishes in a wide variety of soils, but it does require humus in some form. Loosen the soil to a spade's depth, adding compost or leaf mold if necessary. Turn the soil and compost, and then set the rhizomes horizontally, rootlets down, at a depth of two and a half to three inches. Cover the rhizomes with soil, tamp lightly, and water.

Left undisturbed, healthy plants will successfully self-seed.

If, however, you want to increase your colony quickly, dig up the rhizomes and divide so that there are one or two buds per division, then plant the divisions as when transplanting. Plants begun in this way frequently won't bloom until the following year.

To prolong the blooming period of your bloodroot colonies, plant rhizomes in a variety of locations—the cooler and shadier the site, the later the bloom. Set one colony at the base of a south-facing stone wall, for example. These plants will bloom early because the stones retain the sun's heat, thus warming the soil more quickly than would be true of shadier sites. By experimenting over a period of years, you may find a variety of locations for colonies and thereby prolong the blooming season for up to three weeks.

GROWING FROM SEED

The second way to propagate bloodroot in the garden is to gather the seed pods when they mature. In the Northeast, for example, that would be in late June or early July. Store the seeds in a cool, dry place; then, in late summer, plant them one-half-inch deep in a cold frame. The soil mixture should be half leaf mold and half sand. Once the seeds are planted, cover the soil with an inch of milled sphagnum moss. The seeds will germinate the following spring. Transfer the seedlings to their permanent location when the single leaf is about an inch across. Seedlings started this way will not bloom until the second or third year.

The third method is to purchase the exquisite double blood-root, a form of the single. It is for this third alternative that all gardeners owe thanks to Guido von Webern. He left that colony of fully doubled bloodroot intact for three years, by which time it had multiplied to the point at which he could safely divide the plants. He sent a specimen to the Arnold Arboretum, and in the 1923 issue of *Gardener's Chronicle* E. H. Wilson named the 48-petaled mutation *Sanguinaria canadensis* var. *multiplex* so as to distinguish it from the 14-to-16-petaled variety *flore pleno* mentioned in 1732 by Dellenius.

The double bloodroot is unlike the single in three respects. It's a sterile plant, it can have 64 petals rather than 8 to 12, and it has a heavier rhizome and leaf than the single form. Because it's sterile, the double cannot survive without regular division. If left alone, as was von Webern's colony after his death, these plants develop such a large and lifeless pithy section at the tail end of the rhizome that a colony will eventually crowd itself to the surface, where it will dry out and die.

Bloodroot colonies should be divided every three or four years. After the leaves have died back, lift the rhizomes with a fork, break off the pithy sections, and reset the younger, viable portions of the rhizomes 8 to 10 inches apart in soil enriched with leaf mold.

Von Webern's colony died around 1966, and the fate of the rhizome sent to the Arnold Arboretum is unknown. Where, then, did the present rhizomes originate? That question puzzled H. Lincoln Foster, a prominent horticulturist from Falls Village, Connecticut, and in the early 1970s he began a search for the parent of today's plants. He discovered that von Webern had given rhizomes to two other friends. One of these rhizomes was known to have died. However, the fate of the second was unknown as far as Foster could determine through personal correspondence.

Undaunted, Foster wrote an article for the *American Horticultural Society Bulletin* asking if any readers might know what happened to that second rhizome. Henry Teuscher, director emeritus of the Montreal Botanical Gardens, identified himself as the recipient of the other division. Furthermore, he had propagated and distributed many divisions to horticulturists in America and abroad. In so doing, he had assured a future for the plant that Guido von Webern discovered one warm spring day more than 70 years ago.

14

EPIMEDIUM

Epimedium is a handsome, tough, and versatile perennial. Over the years I've used it or seen it used in many ways: as a groundcover under spring-blooming trees or shrubs; as an accent or filler plant at the edge of a garden in filtered shade; as a single specimen in the rock garden; massed at the base of a shady wall; in woodlands; or, appropriate to its Far Eastern origins, in a Japanese garden.

Epimedium's elegance derives partly from its curious columbine-like flowers that bloom in late spring or early summer, but primarily from its handsome foliage which, in early spring, unfurls to form a 12-inch-high clump of dense, light-green leaves with prominent red streaking. By early summer the offset heart-shaped leaves turn a glossy, darker green and remain beautifully veined or edged with red throughout the summer. In autumn the leaves, which persist through the winter, turn bronze. In the warmer zones, foliage might even remain evergreen.

Bishop's hat, one of epimedium's common names, refers to the biretta-like shape of the flower, which has petals, sepals, and a spur. These flowers, held in airy clusters just beyond the foliage on wiry stems, range in color from white through creams and yellows, to pinks and deep reds. The flowers differ from species to cultivar in size as well as color. In many the flower stems don't extend past the foliage by more than two or three inches. (The plant's other common name, barrenwort, refers to the use of its roots in eighteenth- and nineteenth-century decoctions that supposedly prevented conception.)

In the wild, the approximately 25 species of this member of the barberry (Berberidaceae) family are woodland dwellers primarily from China and Japan, though some are native to southern Europe and North Africa. In America, they are hardy in Zones 3 through 8 and, as in their native habitats, prefer a

moist, acidic, highly organic soil that allows rhizomes to spread
easily. Epimedium seems to grow best in partial shade but will
tolerate full shade. (Shady locations are definitely preferable
where summers are hot, but it will do well in sun where soil is
deep and moist.) It will also tolerate extremely dry conditions.
In my garden it grows even under maple trees, which have
voracious surface roots. The plants don't prosper there, I has-
ten to add, but they did survive the very dry summer of 1988
when even several drought-tolerant hostas were struggling.

Where epimedium does prosper is in a spring garden my
wife and I planted in the filtered shade and always moist soil
under a copse of wild plum trees that were on our property
when we bought it. I pruned the dead lower limbs of the plums
up seven or eight feet to allow easy passage under them. After
clearing brambles and saplings from under the trees I forked
loads of well-decomposed cow manure and peat into the soil.
Now every spring the tops of the 15-foot-high wild plums
bloom to create a cloud of white blossoms hovering over our
spring garden.

Three years ago I bought several five-pint containers of *Epimedium* × *rubrum*, each of which cost around $5. I planted
seven of them in a drift along the edge of the stone path
through our spring garden. I set them in soil I had amended
with a wheelbarrow-load of four-year-old sheep manure compost (because I have a truckload of it) and within an existing
planting of *Iris cristata, Bergenia cordifolia*, European ginger (*As-
arum europaeum*), *Digitalis* × *mertonensis, Primula japonica*, maidenhair fern (*Adiantum pedatum*), *Hosta* 'Krossa Regal', and leop-
ardsbane (*Doronicum grandiflorum*). This created a combination
of plants that worked together both in harmonious color combinations of flower and interesting contrasts of foliage type and
texture. Because *E.* × *rubrum* spreads very slowly (much more
slowly than *E. sulphureum*, for example), I set the plants about
eight inches apart. Only after three years are they beginning to
fill in.

OTHER USES

Francis Rohr, a Vermont gardening friend who introduced me
to epimedium many years ago, uses *E.* × *rubrum* as a ground-

cover under a pruned, tree-shaped version of shadblow (*Amelanchier canadensis*). I've also seen it used under magnolias and many spring-blooming shrubs.

Because the leaves don't begin to unfurl until after the miniature early-spring bulbs are in bloom, interplanting epimediums with large-flowering crocuses, winter aconite, *Scilla sibirica*, and the common snowdrop is very successful. After the bulbs bloom the leaves of the epimediums come up to hide the unsightly foliage that follows.

I've also seen epimedium combined in broad drifts in partial or filtered shade with *Bergenia cordifolia* and liriope in front of an ornamental grass such as fountain grass (*Pennisetum alopecuroides*).

If you have little time but want an elegant garden, you can site crabapple trees in front of a stone wall and underplant them with drifts of *Lamium* 'Beacon Silver', *Vinca minor* 'Bowles', *Lamiastrum* 'Herman's Pride', ivies, and any of the epimediums noted below.

Epimedium could also be a component in a garden at the front of the house that would be an alternative to typical foundation planting and lawn. Asymmetrically, 10 to 15 feet from the house, you could put a *Cornus florida* and a *Malus floribunda* on either side of the walk leading to the front door. Then, nearer the house, plant dwarf yew (*Taxus cuspidata* 'Nana'), a thornless firethorn (*Pyracantha coccinea* 'Lalandei Thornless'), and Wilson's rhododendron (*Rhododendron × laetevirens*). As groundcover under the shade of trees and shrubs you could plant blue-flowering *Vinca minor* 'Bowles' and the white form 'Gertrude Jekyll', *Anemone hupehensis*, and *Epimedium × rubrum*. (Because epimedium is slow to spread, set out plants you hope to use as groundcover 10 to 15 inches apart, depending on the size of the initial plants.)

Next summer I plan to use *Epimedium × versicolor* 'Sulphureum', the most drought-tolerant of the epimediums, as part of a garden I designed that is Japanese in spirit. The centerpiece will be a Japanese black pine (*Pinus thunbergii*), underplanted with a single bloodleaf Japanese maple (*Acer palmatum* 'Atropurpureum'), both of which will be sparsely interplanted with *Ilex crenata* 'Helleri'. I'll set groupings of large lichen-covered rocks among these shrubs and trees and then

With spade-shaped leaves and red, violet, white, or yellow flowers, epimedium is an attractive groundcover that thrives in organically rich soil in full or partial shade. Combine it with blue-flowering pulmonaria and yellow primroses in front of a pink-flowering azalea.

plant the 'Sulphureum' in groups and as single plants in relation to the groups of stones.

IMPORTANT SPECIES, FORMS, AND CULTIVARS

Here are some of the epimediums you may want to consider for your garden, with descriptions of size, color, and availability.

E. *alpinum* (Alpine barrenwort): native to southern Europe; to 12 inches; flowers one-half inch wide, sepals red, petals yellow, slipper-like, spurs short so that it looks like a small spurless columbine; E. × *rubrum*, with red flowers, and E. × *rubrum* 'Luteum', with yellow flowers. (Very rare commercially, often labeled E. *alpinum* when it's probably E. × *rubrum*, its hybrid with E. *grandiflorum*).

E. *grandiflorum* (also known as E. *macranthum* or longspur epimedium): from Japan, Manchuria, Korea; to 12 inches; flowers, held above leaves 8 to 10 inches, shaped like Bishop's hats, one or two inches wide, appearing mid to late spring; outer sepals red, inner sepals violet, petals white, spurs prominently projecting to one inch; half-evergreen leaves, thin and leathery, to three inches long, in clusters of three on wiry stems; red-bronze as they unfold and again in autumn. This is the parent of many of the hybrids that have flowers in loose sprays, generally larger and brighter than those of other species or cultivars. Cultivars (rare in commerce): 'Violaceum', with inner sepals and petals light violet; 'Rose Queen', with silvery pink flowers; 'White Queen', with silvery white flowers; 'Yenomoto', semidouble flowering form of 'White Queen'; 'Aureum', a light-yellow-flowered form, 12 inches tall in dry soil but taller in moister, richer soils, found wild recently in Japan.

E. *perralderianum*: from Atlas Mountains of Algeria; 12 to 18 inches; a pyramid of yellow butterfly-like flowers on a 12- to 18-inch stem; young leaves are bright green with bronze-red markings, gradually turning to copper-bronze in winter; the only true evergreen epimedium; nearly indistinguishable from E. *pinnatum*.

E. *pinnatum* (yellow barrenwort): from northern Iran and Caucasus; to 12 inches; brilliant yellow, red-spurred flowers on an orchid-like spike; nearly evergreen foliage; this supplies the yellow color to the genus and hybrids; a vigorous spreader, and thus good as a groundcover but not often seen in commerce.

E. × rubrum (red barrenwort): from Japan; 9 to 12 inches, flowers opening in June to one inch across, inner sepals bright crimson, petals pale yellow or white tinged with red; slipperlike, spurs slightly upcurved; leaves open red-bronze, then turn to green with a margin of red throughout the season; a cross between *E. alpinum* and *E. grandiflorum*; the most common in commerce, and most floriferous; a choice plant.

E. × versicolor: to 12 inches; flowers in June nearly one inch across, inner sepals rose, petals yellow, spurs tinged with red; leaves mottled or red when young, later green. Cultivars: 'Sulphureum', leaves usually not mottled, inner sepals pale yellow, petals brighter yellow and it is the fastest spreading and perhaps the most drought-tolerant and graceful of all; 'Neosulphureum', inner sepals creamy-yellow, petals lemon-yellow, spurs short, tinged brown; 'Warleyensis', to 10 inches, a strong-growing hybrid with large two-toned flowers copper and yellow. 'Warleyensis' appeared spontaneously in Ellen Willmott's garden at Warley Place in England. She would never give anyone a starter plant but guarded it closely all her life, through decades of visiting garden clubs. It eventually was introduced.

E. × youngianum (Young's barrenwort or snowy epimedium): from Japan; to one foot; flowers white or rose, to 1¾ inch across and pendulous; hybrid of *E. grandiflorum* and *E. diphyllum*. Cultivars: 'Niveum', with pure white flowers (sometimes listed as 'Album') is a choice, slow-grower to eight inches, after six years it might be a foot wide; 'Roseum', to eight inches, with rose-lilac flowers.

Dividing the rhizomes

Epimediums are so easily propagated by division that I've never tried seed propagation. Just after they bloom, or in the early spring, I fork the plants with their relatively shallow rhizomes out of the ground and lay the clumps on a plastic ground cloth. With my hands, I break the plant with its rhizomatous system into small clumps. If you need a lot of plants, divisions can be as small as one thin wiry stem connected to a section of rhizome, and you could get 20 or more of those from a plant in a five-pint container. I transplant these in semishade in a rich, organic soil I've prepared with generous amounts of well-decomposed cow manure and peat. Then I water them well.

Epimediums are long-lived and generally slow-spreading. They can remain in one site for a long time with a minimum of maintenance. The only time they require attention is in the early spring. Using hedge shears, I cut the stems of the spent leaves from the previous season to about an inch above ground level before new growth starts. (I don't cut the leaves off in autumn because they add visual interest to the garden and also tend to hold snow, protecting leaf and flower buds through the winter.)

Disease- and pest-free, low-maintenance, versatile in the landscape, useful throughout two-thirds of America, long-lived, noninvasive, refined flowers, elegant foliage—what more could we ask of a perennial?

15

BAPTISIA

Baptisia australis is a three- to four-foot-high and -wide herbaceous perennial that can play many roles in the landscape. Its restrained nature makes it compatible with countless shrubs and perennials. In Zones 3 through 8, it can be planted in the middle of a perennial border, in a cutting bed for its indigo-blue (albeit fleeting) flowers and blue-green foliage, as part of a perennial foundation planting, in open areas of woodland, in the herb garden, or as a low hedge, much as peonies are sometimes used. Because *B. australis* is native to dry areas from Pennsylvania south to North Carolina and west to Tennessee, it's naturally drought-tolerant and therefore is a good plant for seaside gardens as well.

The genus *Baptisia* (family Leguminosae) includes some 30 or more species. As a group, they are commonly known as false indigo. The name *Baptisia* derives from the Greek verb *baptizein*, "to dye." Several members of the family, especially the yellow-flowered *Baptisia tinctoria*, yield a sap sometimes used by craftsmen as an inferior substitute for true indigo, which comes from certain species of the also leguminous *Indigofera*. Because *B. australis* is the most common ornamental in the genus, it has been given the generic common name for its own. In some parts of the U.S. it's also known as plains false indigo or wild blue indigo.

Baptisia grows naturally in dry places and will tolerate almost any soil, but it flourishes in an open, humusy ground. It will accept full sun in the northern half of its range but prefers partial shade in warmer climates. At least half a day's sun is necessary to induce blooms, which last only about one week.

TRANSPLANTING

This shrub-like perennial has the deserved reputation for being difficult to transplant because it sends stout roots deep into the ground. It should be planted where it can be left for many years. Having said that, several years ago I bought 10 plants from a local nurseryman. He simply forked the tangle of roots, each about the diameter of a pencil, out of the ground in early spring and dumped them into cardboard boxes. (They can also be purchased in containers.)

I got them back to our garden and dug a half bushel or so of composted manure and peat into sandy soil in full sun, as well as into deep topsoil in both sun and partial shade. I planted the roots one or two inches under the surface and mulched with three to four inches of white pine needles. Every plant is still flourishing.

Because it's a very slow-spreading clump of erect three- to four-foot stems, baptisia can be planted in the middle of a perennial border. It will take three or four years to double the width of its crown, and thus not grow out of bounds. Its fleeting blooms arise at the termini of the upright stems on 8- to 12-inch spikes in late spring or early summer. Butterflies find the blue flowers particularly attractive. In June the blooms combine beautifully with Shasta daisies, red peonies, and sweet William. During the rest of the year the foliage provides a handsome backdrop for any perennials grown near it.

The mound-shaped plant adds stature and mass to a border, providing a backdrop for lower plants such as *Nepeta* × *faassenii* 'Six Hills Giant' (also known as *N. gigantea*), *Achillea* 'Moonshine', *Cerastium tomentosum*, and the annual deep-purple *Heliotropium* × 'Hybrid Marine', which in itself makes a good June combination. These front-of-the-border perennials also hide the leafless lower stems of baptisia. The shrub-like false indigo in turn acts as a screen for the lower stems of back-of-the-border plants such as delphiniums and hollyhocks.

Baptisia's faded flowers gradually transform into dark-brown, hard, plump seed pods that sound like a rattle when disturbed. Baptisia can be easily propagated from seed, though division is simpler and produces large plants much more quickly than seedlings do.

Baptisia is a shrub-like perennial that can be grown in large numbers to form a low, herbaceous hedge, placed as a single accent plant in the perennial border, or used much as a shrub under the eaves of your house, where it will die down in the autumn out of the way of snow from the roof.

Baptisia suffers from no pests or diseases and maintenance is easy. In early summer I push twiggy sticks into the ground around the edge of the plant to help support floppy outer stems. In the autumn, after the first killing frost turns a flourishing plant into a limp black mess almost overnight, I cut what remains to the ground. If I get around to it, I spread three or four inches of well-composted manure right on top of the plant. Division is rarely, if ever, necessary.

16

BEE BALM

If you look into what has been written about bee balm (*Monarda didyma*), the most popular member of its genus, you will find that no one seems to know what horticultural category it belongs in. One authority sees it as an herb with highly aromatic foliage. Another encourages its use as a wild flower. Still others, with their eyes on the parent plant as well as the new cultivars, see it as a flowering perennial, at home with the best in the border. Happily, we don't have to decide, for bee balm is all of these, and that's what makes it so attractive to so many gardeners.

There are 12 species in the genus *Monarda*, so named by Linnaeus in honor of Nicolas Bautista de Monardes (1493-1588), an eminent Spanish physician, botanist, and writer who took great interest in plants arriving on the docks of Seville from the New World.

The two species best known in the garden and the wild are *M. fistulosa*, commonly known as wild bergamot, and the even more familiar *M. didyma*, bee balm. Although both give rise to tight whorls of terminal flowers on two- to three-foot-tall, distinctively square stems through July and August, the flowers of wild bergamot range from light lavender to whitish pink, while those of bee balm are brilliant red. Bergamot grows wild from Maine to Minnesota and south to Florida and Kansas, in the dry sandy soils of hillsides, meadows, roadsides, and prairies. It prefers soil with a pH of 6.5 to 7.5. The range of bee balm is more northerly than that of bergamot. It grows from Quebec and Michigan south to Georgia and Tennessee and prefers moist, highly organic soil with a pH of 5.5 to 6.5. Because bee balm requires the same kind of soil as many other plants that are popular in perennial beds, and because it has such brilliant red flowers, *M. didyma* was the natural choice for hybridizers over the less dramatic *M. fistulosa*.

BIRDS AND TEA

The name bee balm derives from the long-tongued bumblebee's attraction to the bright-red, tubular, mint-scented flowers of *M. didyma*. Since the tongues of most other bees cannot reach all the way into the long, narrow throat of the flower, bumblebees frequently find an unusual abundance of nectar there and are thus especially attracted to it.

Bee balm also attracts the ruby-throated hummingbird. The Audubon Society's *Field Guide to North American Birds* notes that "these smallest of birds are particularly attracted to tubular red flowers such as salvia and trumpet creeper, as well as bee balm, petunia, jewelweed, and thistle." My own experience bears this out. I've seen hummingbirds fly over many varieties of perennials in full bloom, only to stop at a planting of bee balm, where they visit every single flower more than once a day.

If you look carefully at a flower of *M. didyma*, you'll see one reason this plant is so attractive to hummingbirds. The outer end of the tubular flower has a slightly ascending upper lip and a somewhat drooping lower lip, an opening that seems perfectly designed to receive the tiny beak of the hummingbird. The word *didyma*, by the way, means "paired" and refers to the two stamens that protrude with the single pistil from the upper lip. This lip is a characteristic of the family Labiatae, a name derived from *labiate*, meaning "formed like a lip."

Oswego tea is another common name given to *M. didyma* by the early settlers, particularly Shakers, of what is now upstate New York. They found the herb growing there in profusion. The Oswego Indians showed them how to make a minty tea out of the dried flowers and downy leaves.

Just before the flowers reached their peak in early July, the Indians would cut the stems and hang them upside down until dry. They would then strip off the leaves and flowers, dice them, and store a mixture of the two for later use in making an herbal tea. One modern recipe suggests mixing dried *Monarda* leaves with sage or basil (members of the same family) or freshly ground and dried peels of oranges or lemons, or a combination of all four.

Dr. W. J. Hamilton, a septuagenarian gardener and consultant to the Cornell University Plantations in Ithaca, New York, notes that in the 1870s his wife's grandmother used a tea made solely of *Monarda* leaves and flowers for bronchial disorders. After the Boston Tea Party, in 1773, many colonists used *Monarda* and other tisanes (infusions of dried leaves or flowers) when they were forced, for patriotic reasons, to stop drinking imported teas.

PLANT IN MASSES

Bee balm grows naturally in the presence of ferns, since both enjoy moist, highly organic soil. The brilliant red of the bee balm, rivaled in wild flowers only by the cardinal flower (*Lobelia cardinalis*), contrasts in a striking way with the soft green background of Christmas ferns, woodsias, and sensitive or cinnamon ferns. Any of these combinations would be attractive at the edge of a wood or in a moist and shaded or semishaded area within the garden, especially with bee balm planted in bold masses. Cultivars now throw blooms ranging from whites, pinks, and reds to a recently introduced violet-purple called 'Blue Stocking'.

In the shaded, moist areas of his garden in Ithaca, Dr. Hamilton has planted bee balm in company with red and white baneberry (*Actaea rubra* and *Actaea pachypoda*) as well as with hostas. He's also found that bee balm works well with *Lobelia cardinalis* and *Chelone glabra*, turtlehead.

Gertrude Foster, the late author and herb specialist from Falls Village, Connecticut, suggested planting bee balm in an herb garden, particularly behind borage. She found that the furry leaves of borage hide the lower, sometimes relatively leafless parts of the bee balm stem, while the light-blue borage flowers set off the brilliant red of the native bee balm. In fact, the red of these flowers is so brilliant that the Indians called it O-gee-chee, "flaming flower."

This perennial can also make a striking addition to a flower bed when planted in masses at the back of the border. The cultivar 'Adam', with its large, rich cerise-red flower heads, is

Bee balm, attractive to bumblebees and hummingbirds, can be grown in your herb garden, where its leaves can be harvested for tea, or in your perennial border where its bright red flowers can combine with other plants that flower in late June and early July.

particularly well suited for the full-sun border, as it can withstand dry conditions better than the other hybrids. With adequate moisture, any of the other showy cultivars—such as the popular 'Croftway Pink', a hybrid in commerce for over 20 years, 'Cambridge Scarlet', which is reputed to thrive under difficult city conditions, or 'Mahogany'—will do well in full sun. I've planted *M. didyma* near garden loosestrife (*Lysimachia punctata*), Siberian iris, and phlox, all of which enjoy moist soil.

These plants are easy to grow, virtually pest-free, and readily available through most local nurseries or mailorder houses. The hybrids have a hardiness range from Zones 4 to 9, while the species extends that range into Zone 2. Most species will bloom well into August and even early September, provided you cut off the spent blooms. Buds will arise from new stems at the juncture of the next-lower pair of leaves.

Bee balm is sometimes troubled by powdery mildew, which produces a grayish-white powdery coating on leaves and stems. In the Northeast the problem is most acute from late July through August, when cool nights follow warm, humid days. The fungus that forms the mildew lies primarily on the outer surface of the leaves and obtains its food and water through small root-like organs called haustoria that penetrate the epidermal layers of leaf cells. Afflicted leaves are often distorted, curled, or twisted and may be smaller than normal. Late in the season, the gray coating may become dotted with small brown or black specks. Severely infected leaves may yellow and drop off prematurely. The severity of the infection depends on several factors, including air circulation, the age and condition of the plants, and the weather.

You can reduce the chances of infection by planting bee balm plants at least 10 inches apart. This will allow good air circulation between plants. Plant them in an open area rather than at a corner of a building, for example, where air wouldn't circulate well. Don't mulch the plants with leaves or lawn clippings, which attract and hold moisture. Use pine needles instead, as they allow a degree of air circulation at ground level. And don't water the plants excessively. If your plants do become infected, collect and burn damaged leaves and stems to destroy the overwintering stages of the fungus.

You can prevent the growth of powdery mildew by spraying

the leaves and stems with Karathane, sulfur, benomyl, or Ortho Systemic Rose and Floral Spray. Apply any of these weekly beginning in mid July, before the mildew has a chance to get established. Continue weekly applications through the end of August. If you have a bad infestation of mildew and you don't want to use fungicides, you can cut the stems back three or four inches as late as the third week in July and you may still see blooms before the growing season ends.

DIVIDE REGULARLY

Many gardeners and seedsmen complain about the rampant growth of bee balm. They say that it's invasive, that it requires some control. I haven't found this to be a serious problem because the root systems are so shallow that unwanted plants are easy to uproot. Simply take hold of the stems of those plants you don't want and pull them up.

Bee balm is invasive because of the way it reproduces vegetatively. Just as the blooms peak in midsummer, the buds of stolons, or runners, begin to form around the base of each stem, an inch or so below the surface of the soil. The buds form at the joint between the base of the stem and the upper part of the root system. As is true with heleniums, chrysanthemums, and some boltonias, the buds of bee balm grow outward into stolons several inches long. By September or early October, as many as 20 plantlets may be radiating from the parent stem on white, three- to four-inch stolons. Depending on soil, climate, and temperature, little leaves may form at the very tips of these stolons before the onset of heavy frosts. (So that you won't damage the stolons, pull weeds by hand around bee balm.)

Because each stem gives rise to so many new plants every season, plants require periodic division. If left untended, a crown of bee balm can overcrowd itself in three or four years and begin to die back in the center.

In early spring, just before the young plants begin their active growth, take a sharp spade and cut pie-shaped pieces out of the crown, leaving a generous section in place. Once you have lifted the divisions, cut out the older inner portions that appear root-bound or dead. Then set out the healthy, young divisions 12 to 18 inches apart in enriched, moist soil. These divisions will take hold without much ado. If your soil dried out quickly, mulch the transplanted divisions with two or three inches of pine needles to help keep the moisture level high. Once the plants are established, you can remove the pine needles.

Another way to introduce bee balm into your garden is to plant the seeds in early fall. You can order seeds by mail or collect them yourself in late September from your own plants. Cover the seeds with a half-inch of soil and then mulch lightly with pine needles. Remember that seeds collected from hybrids will not necessarily come true to color. Only those from the species are truly predictable.

If you'd like to help these plants return to the woods in the profusion with which they originally grew, you might do what Dr. Hamilton does. In late autumn or early spring, when he knows he'll be walking near the edge of woodlands or fishing for trout along shady streams, he takes along packets of bee balm seeds. When he comes upon damp, rich, friable soil in shade or semishade, he plants the seeds. Now and again he goes back to check on his plantings out there in the wild, and invariably finds that they have grown into healthy, bright colonies.

17

CATMINT

Catmint's uses go well beyond amusing cats. I was unaware of all the possibilities of this plant until my wife and I visited public and private gardens in England several years ago. There we saw it used in various ways, invariably to good effect. Because of their soft silver-green foliage and spikes of lavender florets, the best catmints (*Nepeta* species) can be used among other fine ornamental plants to pull disparate colors and textures together in harmonious ways.

There are at least three catmints that you should know about. *Nepeta cataria*, the true catmint, or catnip, is a coarse, two- to three-foot-high and -wide herb that is indeed a feline favorite. But catnip is not a plant for ornamental borders, in part because it's such a rampant self-seeder, but also because it's not as attractive as other members of the genus. It could be planted in an herb garden or a child's garden, where cats will delight children with their mindless rolling, especially in leaves that have been bruised. Like that of the other two nepetas, catnip foliage is silvery green and highly aromatic (it has a minty scent and flavor). It should be harvested to dry for teas or cat toys when the flowering starts in early summer. If cats become a nuisance as they roll in this or the other nepetas, place a few thorny twigs of rose or barberry in the planting to discourage them.

CLASSIC EDGING PLANTS

The catmints of greatest horticultural interest are *N. mussinii* and *N. × faassenii*. When you begin looking for these plants you'll find a confusion in nomenclature—they're frequently regarded as synonymous. It's safe to say that the former is a species whereas the latter is a hybrid, a cross between *N. mussinii* and *N. nepetella*.

Regardless of nomenclature, both are superior, large-scale plants for the garden. *N. mussinii* is a 1½- to 2-foot-high, spreading (though by no means invasive) perennial. Gertrude Jekyll used it in association with other gray-green-leaved plants such as *Cerastium*, *Echinops*, *Stachys lanata*, and *Santolina*. I've seen catmint combined with *Artemesia*, *Centaurea cyanus*, *Dianthus*, *Limonium latifolium*, *Lavandula*, and *Veronica incana*.

There is a more compact cultivar of *N. mussinii* called 'Blue Wonder'. It's 10 to 15 inches tall and forms a uniform, spreading mound of tiny leaves, covered with six-inch flower spikes in spring and early summer. We have 12 of these along the top of a low stone retaining wall on the south side of our gray clapboard house. We interplanted them with large-flowering and species crocuses. Behind the catmints and crocuses we set seven Russian sages (*Perovskia atriplicifolia*), two- to three-foot-high, silver-leaved, fragrant plants that throw tall spires of lavender-blue flowers later in summer. Last spring we introduced 15 to 20 *Achillea taygetea* 'Moonshine' and a similar number of *Dianthus gratianopolitanus* among the catmint to create an interesting interplay of red, yellow, and lavender flowers, a combination made coherent by various shades and textures of the gray-green foliage common to all the plants.

The most dramatic of the catmints is *N. × faassenii* 'Six Hills Giant' (*N. gigantea*, according to some authorities), a plant named after Clarence Elliott's Six Hills Nursery in Hertfordshire, England. This sterile hybrid is larger and hardier than *N. mussinii*, and can tolerate a less well-drained soil. In England we saw plants that were two and sometimes three feet across, growing in semishaded soil. We also visited Tintinhull House, a British National Trust property in Somerset, where Penelope Hobhouse, an expert on color, does her gardening. In a horticultural *tour de force*, she uses this cultivar as a dramatic edging along the walks in the vegetable garden. The honey-colored gravel of the paths, as well as the greens of lettuces and zucchini, associate surprisingly well with the catmint's flower and foliage.

Because the blooms of 'Six Hills Giant' are a soft blue, it can be combined successfully with many perennials. If you already

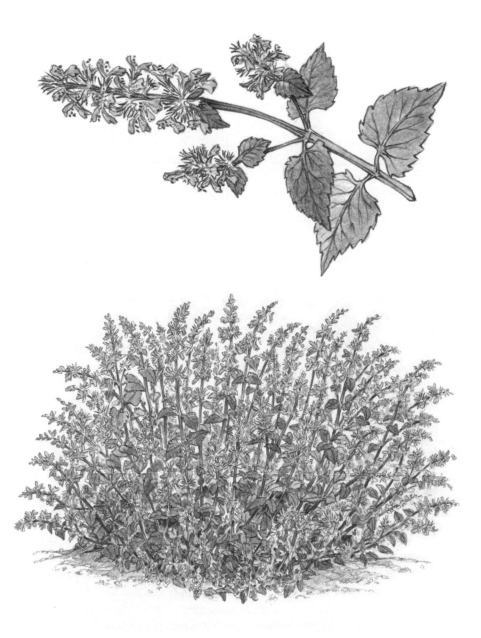

Catmint's long-lasting, lavender flowers make a satisfying early-summer perennial combination with the red of bee balm, the pastel yellow of coreopsis, and the pink of dianthus.

have bearded irises or pink poppies and peonies in your garden, for example, clumps of this catmint planted among or in
front of any of these would satisfy. Catmint in all its forms is
also the classic edging plant for roses; catmint with *Rosa rugosa*
'Blanc Double de Coubert' is an especially satisfying and fragrant combination. Or use it as part of a blue garden with such
perennials as *Delphinium, Anchusa, Salvia patens,* and *Galtonia.*
Hobhouse notes in her book, *Color in Your Garden,* that "the
low-toned silver-green foliage can also be used to increase the
dazzling effects of any red, orange, or hard yellow. Gray makes
pure rich hues as brilliant as is possible. Bright orange flowers
can be colored incidents in a sea of pale-blue catmint."

SHEARING AND DIVIDING

Catmints prefer a well-drained (never heavy) soil in full sun.
However, *N.* × *faassenii* can tolerate a moister soil and more
shade than *N. mussinii.* Both grow well in Zones 3 through 8,
though the hybrid is the hardier of the two. We saw 'Six Hills
Giant' in bloom as late as mid July in a corner of a Cotswold
garden that received only three or four hours of midday sun.

   N. mussinii and *N.* × *faassenii* bloom for two or three weeks
starting in mid June, and they bloom a second time if sheared.
Shearing (use hedge trimmers) is also necessary to prevent the
plant from becoming floppy and a bit shabby looking later in
the season. Katherine Marshall-Mathisen, who until 1984 su-
pervised the Wall Garden at Old Westbury on Long Island,
looked after 75 feet of catmint hedges that edge mixed perennial borders there. In early April, when new shoots were six or
eight inches tall, she sheared the top three inches off to produce a more compact and floriferous plant. Immediately after
the best of the bloom was over around mid June, she sheared
the plants back halfway. "When you first shear them back," she
says, "they look like you gave them a crew cut, but in two
weeks or so the foliage comes back to produce a fuller, nicer-
looking plant." In late August or early September the plants
bloom again. To prevent mice from overwintering, she sheared
the plants down to within two or three inches of the ground in
early November.

   Catmints are easy, reliable plants, untroubled by pests save the aforementioned cats. Dividing their crowns every two or three years in late autumn or early spring keeps the plants vigorous and hardy. Indeed, division is the best means of propagating this superior and versatile perennial, one that Gertrude Jekyll said "can hardly be overpraised."

ROSES

You may have thought about planting roses in your garden but found them daunting. There seems to be so much to learn about plant choice, hardiness, planting, and maintenance. For advice, I turned to Mike Lowe of Nashua, New Hampshire, an expert on old garden roses. If you want to grow roses, the primer that follows should help.

18 🌹

RUGGED ROSES

The rose, voted America's national flower, is an essential element in our picture of the perfect flower garden. We who garden in the North, like gardeners further south, want to be able to raise ramblers that become cascades of pink blooms in June. We want to plant shrub roses near the front door that, come early July, are covered with so many blooms that their fragrance fills the front room. We want to have vases of our roses on the table, and a bouquet of delicate blooms to give our friends when we go visiting on Sunday afternoon.

But it wasn't until I talked with Malcolm Lowe at his garden in Nashua, New Hampshire, that I realized that gardeners in the northern tier of North America can choose from hundreds of wonderful roses. They aren't the relatively tender, demanding, yet popular hybrid teas and floribundas that we see in page after page of glossy garden catalogs. They are mostly the old garden roses—the eglantines, albas, centifolias, gallicas, rugosas, Bourbons, moss, and species roses. And we have to order them from specialty nurseries that put out mimeographed 12-page lists with a few line drawings. We can also pick from the more recently introduced pillar and shrub roses.

It's the hybrid teas and floribundas, which receive such wide national attention in the gardeners' columns and garden catalogs, that have given northern gardeners the impression that roses are delicate, finicky plants not worth the bother. After all, June is rich with peonies and poppies, irises and daylilies, lupins and foxgloves. Why introduce demanding roses into their midst?

Lowe's rose garden, however, dispelled all the preconceptions I had about roses. Not only are there hundreds of lovely and fragrant roses that are hardy in Zones 2 through 5, but their natural hardiness is enhanced even further by innovative products that will get them through the winter. And old garden roses are generally much less susceptible to pests and diseases than the teas and floribundas. Gardeners don't need to use toxic chemicals to keep their roses looking good. In fact, Lowe notes that dilute Lysol and good cultural practices can take care of most pests and diseases. Furthermore, old garden roses require minimal pruning and thinning.

But what we sacrifice for ease of cultivation is continuous bloom. "They may not have as long a bloom period as the more popular teas and floribundas," Lowe points out, "but their two- to four-week bloom is far more dramatic. 'Madame Hardy', a damask, can have a thousand blooms within a two-week span, and it's gorgeous!"

Over the past 25 years, Malcolm Lowe, or Mike as he is known in international rose circles, has been an engineer for the Raytheon Corporation. But during that same period, his avocation and abiding passion has been roses and the business he has built around them. Over the years, Lowe and his wife Irene have made collecting trips to England, France, and all over North America to amass their present collection of over 750 old garden roses—roses that predate the introduction of the first hybrid tea in 1867. And, as Lowe points out, many of the old garden roses trace their lineage back to antiquity. "Pliny wrote about the gallicas, and they're hardy to Zone 3. *Rosa alba* is the white rose of York—that's Zone 3 too."

Own-root roses

Lowe's collection of these old roses forms the basis for his mailorder business, Lowe's Own-Root Roses. He sells over 2,000 rooted, as opposed to grafted, plants every year. To propagate plants for his customers, Lowe and many specialty growers like him take cuttings from plants in their gardens during June. He roots the cuttings and lets them mature until they are ready for shipping 17 months later.

The relevance of all this for gardeners in Zones 2 through 5 is that roses grown on their own roots are hardier and longer-lived than the grafted roses in spring catalogs or supermarkets. They can also withstand a broader pH range and more acidic soil. Furthermore, in an open, relatively snowless season, rose plants can die back to the ground. Own-root roses will come back true to name; grafted stock might not. It's also true, though, that these vigorous roses grown on their own roots tend to sucker, the roots traveling underground. Such lack of restraint may be a challenge to tidy gardeners.

WINTERING-OVER

Given New Hampshire's harsh winters, Lowe takes advantage of several recently developed products designed to winter-over roses. Two products—Styrofoam cones two to three feet high, and microfoam sheets, six feet wide and 250 feet long—are among the most important technological advances for those who want to grow roses in the North. Microfoam is closed-cell foam about one-eighth inch thick. "I'm growing roses here that I wouldn't even have dreamed about ten years ago," Lowe told me. "Cones and microfoam enable us to grow many roses one zone further north than ever before. For example, the damasks are hardy into USDA Zone 4, but if you cover them with a rose cone in late fall, their first flush of bloom in June will be the sort that they might get in Zone 5 or 6."

On my visit to Lowe's, he showed me a hybrid Bourbon rose called 'Variegata di Bologna' that he had tied to an eight-foot post to train it as a pillar. "Before microfoam, two-thirds of the plant would die back over the winter. Now each November I wrap it, leaving the top open for air. In the spring it's green to the tips." Not all rose growers leave the cones open during the winter, but it's critical to remove cones in the spring, at the time when forsythia blooms, to prevent diseases.

The general rule for winter protection with cones and micro-foam is simple, Lowe says. "If you're planting a rose one zone north of its known limit, or if you just want to be sure a rose will get through the winter in good condition, protect it. Other-wise, use cones or microfoam only if you want to take the time and spend the money to get unusually fine blooms. Basically, you can leave these old garden roses to their own devices, but be sure to plant with a knowledge of zone limitations. And if you really want to be sure, plant *Rosa acicularis,* the polar rose. That one will bloom *inside* the Arctic Circle. And it's one of the earliest and most fragrant roses."

Rosa rubrifolia, hardy to Zone 2, has delicate, five-petaled, pink blooms. Once the flowers fade, the pink-purple foliage adds great interest until the orange-red hips form. You could plant it within the perennial bed, or in the rose garden underplanted with catmint for a lavender-pink combination.

Lowe showed me the polar rose and hundreds of others. And seeing his roses did more than any conversation could, finally, to erase my doubts about growing roses in the North. There were gallicas with five-inch marbled, striped, or spotted blooms; centifolias, of which Gertrude Jekyll wrote, "No rose surpasses it in excellence of scent"; as well as rugosas and spinosissimas, Chinas and albas, moss roses and ramblers, all in a profusion of bloom.

And where the blooms left off, there were others: *R. rubrifolia* with its subtle gray-pink foliage, *R. alba* with its blue-green foliage, *R. eglanteria*'s apple-scented leaves, and rugosa's and gallica's showy red hips.

If we combine the qualities of hardiness, disease- and pest-resistance, fragrance, ease of care, and deep historical lineage of the old garden roses with new technological advances in rose protection, we gardeners in the North can enjoy any number of roses. They may not repeat across the whole summer the way the hybrids teas do, and they may not have the range of colors—you can hardly find a yellow rose that will grow in Zone 2 or 3—but there are indeed truly fine roses for northern North America.

19

YEAR-ROUND CARE

Where do you site old garden roses and how do you plant them? Should you prune? fertilize? water? Here is rose expert Mike Lowe's calendar for year-round care of these hardy, fragrant, and historic plants.

LATE SUMMER: SITE AND SOIL PREPARATION

Since roses are susceptible to windburn, use trees or walls as breaks against the north wind. If using trees, choose evergreens. Their root systems stay within closer bounds than those of deciduous trees, and they provide a denser windbreak.

Roses do best in full southern sun but can tolerate a minimum of six hours of sun a day. If there is a choice between morning or afternoon shade, choose afternoon. Morning shade, coupled with dew, increases the possibility of mildew and black spot. If possible, choose a site with good air circulation.

Roses like a lot of water throughout the season, but most cannot tolerate poorly drained soil that causes water to stand around their roots. *Rosa palustris*, the swamp rose, is an obvious exception.

Lowe, like all rose experts, is emphatic about the need for careful soil preparation. "If you're going to put a ten-dollar rose in a ten-cent hole, you are better off going to the supermarket and buying a two-dollar rose and hiring a neighborhood kid to dig you an eight-dollar hole."

The home gardener who wants to plant only a few rose bushes should dig holes that are two to three feet deep and wide, saving the topsoil, discarding the subsoil. "Now," Lowe

says, "here's the best way to do this. Once the hole is exca-
vated, put in six inches of topsoil, and six inches of manure
(with sand, if the soil is heavy with clay) along with two or
three handfuls of bonemeal, and a shovelful of wood ash and
lime. Fork it until all the ingredients are well mixed. Then do
the next twelve-inch layer and so on. A lot of texts recommend
adding chemical fertlilizers. Yes, they make the bed a little bit
better but they are not really necessary. After all, a lot of the
chemicals exist naturally in bonemeal and manure." When the
hole is backfilled, mulch and leave the bed to settle while you
wait for the fall delivery of your plants.

If you want to plant a whole bed of roses, follow the same
method, bui "get a backhoe," Lowe suggests not at all face-
tiously, and follow the same method as above. Liming requirements will vary depending on the soil—roses will do well in
slightly acid to neutral soils.

Lowe's advice on planting is the counsel of perfection. You
don't *have* to dig down 36 inches or even 30 inches. Lowe is an
engineer and he gardens like an engineer. There's another way
to prepare the soil that requires a little less work and is especially good if you find it difficult to get down 30 inches.If a rose
bush is planted at a 45-degree angle, its roots will travel across
rather than down into the soil. Prepare the soil as described
above but only to a depth of 10 to 15 inches and 6 feet wide.
You can ease the process of soil preparation even further by
raising the bed six inches with landscaping ties, backfilling
with prepared soil. Insulate the back of any retaining wall that
is seven inches deep or more with two-inch-thick closed-cell
Styrofoam.

In a 6-foot-wide bed, plant the first row 1 foot from the front,
and 18 inches on center, with the roots fanned out on a 45-
degree slope facing toward the back of the bed. Then plant a
second row 1 foot from the back of the bed, again placing each
on a 45-degree angle. These plants should also be 18 inches on
center, with their roots fanned toward the front and between
pairs of roses in the front row. If you really want to do it right,
place an irrigation line down the center of this bed with a
nozzle every two feet or so. To hold down mildew and black
spot, it's best to water roses at ground level rather than at leaf
level.

FALL: PLANTING

Plant roses in the fall. Since rose plants continue to develop roots as long as the soil isn't frozen, they'll go into the spring with an established root system. The problem with spring planting is that the bush doesn't have time to develop a sound root system before leafing out and is thus more susceptible to disease, insects, and fungus.

And roses can be transplanted very late in the autumn, or even early winter. As Lowe says, "I can remember receiving thirty roses on December 13 one year. I put up a plastic tent over the beds and put a barn heater inside the tent to thaw the ground. Once thawed, I planted the roses, put cones on top of them, and took down the tent. The following spring I found I had lost only one; the rose cone had blown off. There is only one rejoinder to late fall planting: Don't let any frozen soil drop into the hole so that it can come in contact with rootlets. It will kill them."

If you cannot plant immediately upon receiving your order, heel the plants in at a 45-degree angle in a trench, and then water and mulch. Lowe recommends placing them in a bucket of water for at least six hours before planting. "In fact, I have planted dormant roses after they've been in a bucket of water for three weeks, and they did fine."

When planting in either previously prepared individual holes or beds, dig a wide, 10-inch-deep hole. Then place a three-by-three-inch square of broken plasterboard in the bottom of the hole. This will be a ready source of lime for five or six years. Backfill with two to three inches of prepared soil and set in the plant.

The crown of an own-root plant should be one inch below the surface. With grafted plants, the lower the zone number, the deeper the crown: Zone 2–3 inches, Zone 3–2 inches, Zone 4–1 inch. Those gardening in Zones 2 to 3 should seriously consider planting only own-root roses. Those in Zone 4 can plant grafted roses as well. Do not withhold water in the fall–the real winter enemy of roses is desiccation, not cold temperatures.

Gardeners in more temperate climates are always encouraged to prune their roses back severely when planting. Not so in the North. Except for broken roots, do not prune shoots or roots when planting new roses. Prune broken roots just above the break.

EARLY WINTER: WATER AND PROTECTION

If there's a dry spell, water. Once the soil has frozen to a depth of about one-half inch—in Zone 4 that's typically just after Thanksgiving—place winter protection over the roses. Lowe suggests using either the Styrofoam rose cones or bushel baskets. If you use wooden baskets, wrap microfoam around the outside to prevent wind from getting at the plant.

When using rose cones, cut a three-inch-diameter hole in the top to provide some air circulation. Tie up the plant before sliding the cone over it. Place a brick or stone on top of the cone, leaving the hole partially open.

Before rose cones were developed, the standard winter rose protector was the 10-inch-high earth mound around the base of the plant, but Lowe finds gardeners run the risk of gathering too much moisture around the plant. "If the soil is sandy and not too wet, it's okay. I've found heavy soils cause dieback, but then, other people I know use the earth-mound method, and it works well for them."

EARLY SPRING: PRUNING AND SPRAYING

It is critical to remove the rose cones or soil mounds when the forsythia and early daffodils are in bloom so as to prevent disease. The best way to remove soil mounds is to take off as much as you can by hand and then gently hose off what remains.

For young plants set out the previous fall, most old garden roses need little if any pruning, but if you find dead and broken branches, prune them off just after you remove the winter protection. Two weeks later, when the bud-eyes start to sprout and before they leaf out, cut out any dead growth you missed first time around and shape the plant if it needs it. Remember, whatever you cut has flower buds on it. For established plants, it helps to understand what type of wood gives rise to flowers. Damask perpetuals, moss, and rugosa roses bloom on new and old wood. Damask, albas, centifolias, gallicas, and species roses bloom on second-year wood. *Rosa foetida* blooms on third-year wood. Prune accordingly.

Another general rule for pruning old garden roses, according to Lowe, is, "If you want larger flowers on a medium-sized plant, cut back one-third. If you want lots of medium-sized flowers on a large bush, leave the plant alone." Ramblers should only be pruned after they have flowered.

When pruning to shape a rose plant, make cuts just above an outward-facing bud. This results in better aeration, a deterrent to fungal disease, because the branching grows outward, creating a looser, more open plant. Collect all the prunings and burn them to destroy any fungi or insect eggs.

If you had a lot of mildew, black spot, or spider mites the previous season, which is far less likely than if you were growing the fancy hybrid teas and floribundas grown in warmer climates, spray with dilute Lysol (one tablespoon per gallon of water). If you need to spray rugosas for fungi and insects, now is the time to do it, because they resent spraying once their leaves are out.

SPRING: FERTILIZING AND PEST PREVENTION

Depending on soil pH, add lime, as well as two cups of well-balanced organic fertilizer to ensure a healthy spring surge and to encourage good bud formation. Spread the lime and fertilizer on the surface of the soil and then lightly scratch in with a rake to avoid damaging surface roots. Follow up with a good soaking. Then spread two to three inches of well-decomposed cow manure to maintain rich, moist soil.

Spray dilute Lysol on the plants weekly if you have a persistent mildew problem. To prevent further problems, don't plant roses near mildew-prone plants like bee balm, phlox, or lilacs. If combining roses with perennials, be sure the perennials are low-growing so they don't impede air circulation. For treatment of black spot, spread wood ashes liberally around the plant, but if the problem persists, take the time to pick off the affected leaves and burn them.

"When all else fails," says Lowe, "water." During prolonged periods of drought, thoroughly soak the soil at least twice a week or more, depending on the water-holding capacity of the soil. "The best time to water is early morning so that when the sun hits the leaves and transpiration begins in earnest there will be plenty of water then and throughout the day."

To control Japanese beetles, place a yellow bucket 20 or 30 yards from the roses, and then place a few peaches or other fleshy fruits in the bottom in a couple inches of soapy water. The beetles will find their way to the bucket and fruit, and many will drown in the water.

To combat earwigs, spray them directly with dilute Lysol or collect them and the Japanese beetles in the morning when they are inactive.

You know you have an infestation of spider mites if the undersides of the leaves look dirty. A magnifying glass will enable you to see them. Soapy water will kill spider mites but you must spray the tops and bottoms of the leaves every three to four days. Three or four applications usually suffice.

SUMMER AND EARLY FALL: MAINTENANCE

If established plants are getting too big, cut them back after they bloom. "Why waste flowers?" Lowe says. Also prune out old weak canes that are not producing abundant leaves. Continue watering and spraying for any pests and fungi that persist.

Many bushes die from neglect in the early fall. Don't spread wood ash or lime in the fall because elevating the pH releases nitrogen into the soil, thus bringing on leaf growth that's susceptible to the autumn frosts. And don't let the soil dry out. To help the plants harden off for the winter, allow hips to form, and refrain from cutting flowers or pruning new and established bushes.

20 🌺

CHOOSING OLD
GARDEN ROSES

How do you choose among the hundreds of lovely and fragrant old garden roses? For plants hardy in Zones 2 through 4 (or those hardy only in Zones 5 and 6 that you plan to protect), expert Mike Lowe recommends buying species roses before any others. "If I could have only thirty roses, I would choose thirty species. They're hardier, and in almost all cases, the most beautiful of their type."

Here are Lowe's recommendations and advice on choosing old garden roses. Unless otherwise noted, these roses bloom once—in June through early July—for a period ranging from two to four weeks. The types are listed with a general introduction, followed by selected hardy varieties. The date of introduction follows each specific plant—in general, the earlier that date, the hardier the plant. "With protection" means that microfoam should be wrapped around the taller plants, and rose cones placed over the base of the smaller ones.

ALBAS

These are tall (to eight feet or more), dense, and upright with especially handsome bluish-gray foliage. They make good background plants for smaller roses or perennials. This "capital rose, a great favorite in cottage gardens," as Gertrude Jekyll wrote, has been known since A.D. 1200. Some of the roses seen in paintings of the Italian Renaissance can be identified as albas, including the white rose of York.

They come only in white and pink; fragrant; hips long and scarlet; hardy to Zone 3; require little or no pruning. *Rosa* ×

alba 'Semi-plena' (ca. 1600)—semidouble white; 'Chloris' (ca. 1800)—double, light pink, canes thornless; 'Felicite Parmentier' (1834)—good for small garden, light pink with bright rose center; 'Konigin von Danemark' (1826)—pink, double, prickly wood.

BOURBONS

These were discovered on the Isle of Bourbon (now Reunion Island) off the east coast of Madagascar where farmers hedged their fields with the parent China and damask roses. The French collected seeds and plants of this naturally crossbred rose in the early 1800s and developed today's cultivars. According to Lowe, "The hardy hybrids make the best pillars. Tie the nice long canes to lampposts and you'll get great pillar roses with lots of flowers. Because we can't grow the true climbers in Zones 2 through 4, these are the ones to replace them."

Some are repeat bloomers; most have some fragrance; colors range from white to red with white stripes; usually reach six feet or more; most are hardy only to Zone 6 but the following are hardy to Zone 4: 'Coupe d'Hebe' (1840)—rich pink, once-flowering; 'Louise Odier' (1851)—with protection, repeats well, rich pink; 'Variegata di Bologna' (1909)—striped red blend.

CENTIFOLIAS

Known as the cabbage rose in pink, white, and lilac, centifolia's blooms are full-petaled double flowers, the large outer petals enclosing many tightly packed inner petals, often with a button center. Long canes with sparse foliage spring up in all directions, and few centifolias grow into a dense bush. Lowe says, " 'Pompon de Bourgogne' is the best dwarf for hardiness, and you can make it into a sheared hedge." This type is a complex hybrid that developed gradually from the end of the sixteenth century to the beginning of the eighteenth.

R. centifolia (ca. 1600)—the cabbage rose, pink, very fragrant; 'Blanche-fleur' (1835)—double, white, prolific, thick bush; 'Juno' (1847)—cupped, pale pink, a pillar with protection; 'Pompon de Bourgogne' (1664)—rose-pink, small, dense foliage.

CHINAS

The originals are most often dwarf bushes with loosely cup-shaped blooms in pinks and reds that tend to darken rather than fade in sunlight. The blooms shatter cleanly when fully expanded; thus, the early Chinas came to be known as the aristocrats of the roses, because they knew how to die gracefully. They are disease resistant.

Most are hardy only to Zone 5, but the following are hardy in Zone 4: 'Brennus' (1830)—double, bright red, bushy; 'Great Western' (1840)—mauve, a pillar with protection; 'Fulgens' (ca. 1830)—new foliage rust-red, light scarlet bloom.

DAMASKS

With the gallicas and albas, these are considered among the most ancient of roses. Pliny wrote of them, and they were grown in hundreds of monasteries across Europe for medicinal purposes. They come in varying shades of pink to white and are so fragrant they were the traditional source of attar (oil) for perfume. Lowe admits, "There are noses and there are noses, but I think these are the most fragrant roses of all."

They grow five to eight feet with arching, thorny canes; disease resistant; foliage grayish; hips large, round, and red. Hardy to Zone 4, though first flush of bloom will be better if plant is protected. 'Celsiana' (ca. 1750)—to six feet, semidouble, pink to white; 'Four Seasons' (ca. 1790)—to four feet, deep rose, repeats; 'Leda' (1826)—white with crimson edges, red buds.

EGLANTERIAS

Eglantine, or sweetbrier, roses are big 6- to 20-foot plants that can be tied to tall stakes to form pillars. They are once-flowering, but the unusual apple-scented foliage and good hip set pick up where the flowers leave off to make this an attractive plant throughout summer and fall.

Prickly shrubs with small, single, semidouble, and double blooms in white, apricot, pink, red; all hardy to Zone 3. *R. eglanteria* (1551)—light pink, large thorns, large hips; 'Janet's

Pride' (1892)—to five feet, white center; 'Greenmantle' (1859)—
to 20 feet, semidouble, rose-red, white eye.

GALLICAS

Because many of the blooms are spotted, striped, or marbled in
crimson, pinks, and purple, these are commonly known as the
mad gallicas. Cultivated by the Romans, they were the dominant garden rose from the twelfth through the early nineteenth
centuries, including the red rose of Lancaster. They bear fragrant flowers, and fragrance increases as the petals dry.

Hardy, sturdy shrubs three to four feet tall, though there are
larger exceptions; rough foliage, large red hips. The plants
sucker profusely to form dense clumps; prune dead shoots
only. All gallicas hardy to Zone 3. *R. gallica* 'officinalis' (ancient)—'Apothecary's Rose', rose-red; 'Alain Blanchard'
(1839)—crimson, semidouble, mottled darker; 'Belle de Crecy'
(ca. 1830)—deep pink to tones of lavender; 'Charles de Mills'
(ca. 1845)—double, crimson, lighter perimeter; 'La Belle Sul-
tane' (1795)—semidouble, dark crimson, to eight feet; 'Rosa
Mundi' (1581)—semidouble, flaked rose-red with white.

RUGOSAS

"These roses deserve much more attention in the North, because they have all the attributes of toughness," says Lowe.
"They're drought resistant but can also tolerate wet feet. They
tolerate poor soil and many are hardy to minus thirty-five
degrees Fahrenheit. They're disease resistant, and they don't
require spraying—in fact, they resent it. They require no pruning, and there are a lot of new varieties. Look for the range of
rugosas that were developed in Canada over the last ten to
fifteen years and are named after famous Canadian explorers
like Martin Frobisher." Lowe has 26 rugosas in his catalog. "If I
could have only one white rose, it would be *Rosa rugosa* 'Alba'."
Rugosa means wrinkled, referring to the foliage.

Good repeat bloomers with loose, informal single or double
flowers in white, pink, or red and some yellow; four to eight
feet with showy, abundant, tasty red hips. *R. rugosa* 'Alba'
(1870)—large, single, white; 'Jens Munk' (1974)—medium size,

pink, in clusters; 'Rugosa Magnifica' (1905)—semidouble, rose-red; 'Schneezwerg' (1912)—semidouble, small, white, scarlet fruit; 'Will Alderman' (1954)—to four feet, double, rose-pink, clusters; 'Martin Frobisher' (1968)—light pink.

HYBRID SPINOSISSIMAS

"When God created roses, he created these for people living in Zone 2," says Lowe. Many are the earliest roses to bloom in the garden, and they require no tending at all if planted correctly. "The only pruning I do is take out the thirty-year-old wood."

They are also called pimpinellifolia and the Scotch rose; old varieties hardy to Zone 2, modern ones to Zone 4; older varieties seldom exceed five feet; lax, spreading growth habit with fragrant, white and pale pink flowers. *R. spinosissima* 'Lutea' (ca. 1820)—to four feet, medium yellow; 'Dorenbos Selection' (ca. 1950)—dark red, distinct yellow anthers; 'Dominie Sampson' (1848)—small, pink, foliage; 'Harison's Yellow' (1830)—tallest, to eight feet, Zone 3, bright yellow; 'Stanwell Perpetual' (pre-1838)—repeats, white to pale pink.

MOSS ROSES

"I love these and I hate them," says Lowe. "The buds and flowers are gorgeous, but the plants tend not to look as good as the albas or gallicas once they have bloomed, being particularly susceptible to mildew. The moss holds the moisture." They are easily recognized because they form a fragrant, heavy green or reddish-brown prickly moss-like growth on their calyx and stems. The first moss, a mutation of *R. centifolia*, appeared around 1696.

Fragrant, resin-scented flowers are large, fully double and globe-shaped in shades of red, pink, purple, white, stripes; four to six feet; hardy to Zone 3. 'Communis' (1696)—pink, fragrant, longest and mossiest buds; 'Capitaine John Ingram' (1854)—crimson, double, to five feet; 'Mme. de la Roche-Lambert' (1851)—red, good buds, repeats well; 'Rene d'Anjou' (1853)—cupped, deep pink, dark moss, to three feet; 'Salet' (1854)—to five feet, bushy, pink, green moss, repeats well; 'Alfred de Dalmas' (1855)—pale pink to nearly white, repeats.

RAMBLERS

"All the old garden roses bloom until July Fourth and then—bang—they're over," Lowe says. "That's when these come in. And while their individual flowers are not as spectacular as others, their mass effect is fabulous. These are the last hurrah before the midsummer perennial beds take over."

Not truly "old roses," these are big plants that grow as pliable canes from 10 to 30 feet long. As pillars in Zone 4, they have to be wrapped in microfoam or dropped to the ground where snow will cover them. They bloom on two-year-old wood, so prune older wood out to encourage formation of new canes. They have small single or double flowers in large clusters, in pink, red, purple, and white, that bloom late in the season. They like good air circulation. 'American Pillar' (1902)—rose-red with white eye, large hips; 'Dorothy Perkins' (1901)—most popular, pink, double; 'Excelsa' (1909)—bright rose-red, double; 'Veilchenblau' (1909)—to 20 feet, mauve-lavender, best in partial shade.

SHRUBS

These roses, Lowe says, are informal, robust, and repeat flowering. He calls shrub roses "a catchall modern class that has all the attributes of the old garden roses, but which are not as commercially viable if they are so named."

Hardiness and growth habit vary, though most range in height from four to five feet; can be used in herbaceous borders or as hedges. 'Constance Spry' (1961)—large, cupped, pink, Zone 4, to six feet, arching; 'Nearly Wild' (1941)—to three feet, bushy, single pink, constant bloom; 'Prairie Dawn' (1959)—to five feet, Zone 2 with protection, double, pink, repeats well; 'Westerland' (1969)—to eight feet, Zone 4, orange blend, repeats well; 'Scharlachglut' (1952)—to six feet, bright red, single, large hips.

SPECIES AND SPECIES HYBRIDS

"You could fall in love with these plants because they will always give you roses," Lowe says. They are natural, wild roses that grow throughout the northern hemisphere. They all bear single five-petal blooms in all colors, are once flowering, and require virtually no care. They range in height from 2 to 10 feet and are just as wide, so give them room. They bloom on the previous year's wood, so, if you must, prune them shortly after they have bloomed. Hardiness varies.

With species, the year refers only to when first cultivated. *R. acicularis*, the polar rose, Zone 1, fragrant, low growing; *R. canina* (1737)—the dog rose, Zone 3, light pink, 3 to 10 feet, large hips; *R. highdownensis* (1928)—Zone 4, 15 feet, red, large hips; *R. l'heritierana* (1820)—Purple Boursault, crimson-purple, very early; *R. palustris* (1726)—the swamp rose, Zone 2, four to six feet, pink; *R. rubrifolia* (ca. 1800)—Zone 2, two to eight feet, mauve-gray leaves, small, pink, round hips; *R. virginiana* (1752)—Zone 3, three to four feet, medium, pink, glossy leaves, showing fruit, excellent fall color.

TOOLS and TECHNIQUES

When it comes time to actually create your garden, this section will help you think out some of the design decisions—right in the garden. Look closely, for example, at "Edging Tools" when you're making decisions about where and how to lay out the edges of your planting beds. Before doing any work you might want to look at the chapter on garden cloths. It will show you how to use a tarpaulin to save time on initial cleanup. The chapter on work gloves will let you in on a Vermont secret about where to get the best gardening gloves made today. If a section of your garden was planted years ago and has been neglected, there's also a chapter on how to restore that part of your garden. And if you really enjoy pruning and want to get fancy, there's a chapter on pruning espaliered fruit trees.

21

EDGING TOOLS

Clean, crisp lawn edges are worth your time and effort. A tidy edge defines the garden it adjoins and acts as a foil for the flowers and foliage therein. I'm always surprised at the impact newly dug or freshly clipped grass edges have. They make lawns, grass paths, and, of course, gardens look well cared for. They sharpen the image.

A crisp, dropped edge has practical benefits too—it discourages weeds, clover, and the lawn itself from sneaking into a garden. And a lawn with clean edges is easier to mow than one that flows in and out of the garden. Paved edges, whether of brick, cut stone, or fieldstone, are easier to maintain. But to my mind there's nothing so elegant as a lawn edge.

THREE INDISPENSABLE TOOLS

Over the years I've established many edges in my own gardens and in those of my clients, and I've come to use three tools exclusively: a half-moon edging knife, a straight-nosed spade, and a pair of long-handled grass shears. The half-moon edger is indispensable for cutting the turf to establish the edge. This tool comes with a long, straight handle, like that on a hoe, or with a short, stout T-grip handle. Even though I'm six-foot-five, I prefer edgers with T-grips because they are sturdier and because I can push them into the soil by hand rather than by foot. There are fewer movements involved, so the work goes faster. The one I use has a 32-inch ash handle and a four-by-eight-inch carbon-steel blade with no boot tread. Its blade is just the right size to make the uniformly shallow cuts that edging requires. The blade is flat, and I keep it very sharp with a whetstone.

The straight-nosed spade is the best tool for cutting the undersides of turfs (after making the initial cut with the half-moon edger) and then removing them. The edger blade is too small to lift large sods. My spade—a Bantam 2 that was my grandmother's—is 39 inches long with a 12-by-7¼-inch treaded blade and a D-grip handle. It weighs only 3 pounds, 12 ounces, but that's after 60 years of service. It's comparable to the Ames Pony garden spade, for example, except that the Ames spade is a pound heavier. The blade of my spade is thin yet very strong. It holds a keen edge that cuts the undersides of turfs easily. Newer spades I've seen have thicker blades that make them less efficient at slicing, but they'll do the job if their edges are kept sharp on a grinding wheel.

EDGING A FLOWER BED

Two jobs I did—one for a client and one in my own garden—illustrate not only the techniques I've adopted over the years to make and maintain good edges, but also the practical and aesthetic value of such edges.

Years before the client called me, he had planted hybrid daylilies along the front of two 75-foot sections of stone wall that ran on either side of, and perpendicular to, his driveway. The lawn and weeds had subsequently crept in, and, though the daylilies continued to bloom, all was chaos. We cleared the beds of weeds and grass, divided the daylilies, and then set about establishing a clean, straight lawn edge three feet out from the stone walls.

Once I had worked out roughly where the edge would go, I pulled a white cord taut along that line and took measurements out from the stone wall to be sure the edge would parallel the wall. I then set the line firmly at either end. To be sure the cord would stay put as I cut the turf, I pinned it tight to the ground every 10 or 15 feet with four-inch-long, one-inch-wide wire staples. I made these staples out of heavy-gauge wire just for this purpose.

Before I began to cut the turf, I applied some know-how I'd gained from George Cooper, a gardener at Hidcote Manor. He taught me to look closely at the soil to determine the best angle

A neat edge to a lawn path is both practical and aesthetic. With the right tools and techniques, plus a design philosophy, you'll discover that crisply edged lawn paths can move you through your garden in a stimulating way and also help you keep the lawn from invading your beds.

and depth of cut to use. When working in crumbly loam that breaks down underfoot, he advised, set your half-moon edging knife at a 100-degree angle to give the edge more support, and don't dig the edge much deeper than two inches. When working in heavier soil that supports more weight, make a right-angle cut about four inches deep (the full depth of the edger's blade).

Cooper also said to pay attention to the condition of the soil the day you're edging. If the soil along the edge will be adversely affected by your weight as you work—if it's so wet that it will compact, or so dry that it will crumble—find an 8- to 10-foot-long 1-by-4 to stand on as you work. Put the board down next to the cord guide. With both feet, step on the board to hold it steady and then cut along the edge with your half-moon, using only your hands. When you come to the end of the board, leave the half-moon in the ground, move the board along, place the far end up against the blade that's stuck in the ground, and start again. When I come to right angles, I use a straight-nosed spade.

Once I'd made an initial cut the length of the daylily bed with the half-moon edger, I went back to the start and cut the undersides of the sods with my straight-nosed spade, lifted them onto a wheelbarrow, and carted them to a compost pile, where I heaped them upside down. In a year they would make good compost. I then went back and tidied up the edge, moving along its length inserting the edger at the proper angle and to the proper depth, giving the blade a swift kick to send excess soil and debris in under the daylilies.

The edge I dug that day established a clear boundary between lawn and bed, thus improving the bed's health and appearance. Furthermore, the strong horizontal line of the edge was repeated, in turn, by the stone walls, the dirt road behind them, the meadow beyond, and the band of wooded horizon on the far side of the meadow. In the midst of all those strong horizontal lines is a profusion of arching daylily foliage and a changing band of color from June until frost. A coherent image was the result. Order had been established by making a clean, straight edge.

Making a grass path

Curving edges require a slightly different treatment and offer interesting opportunities. One year my wife and I put in a new island bed in full sun. The back side of the bed flowed haphazardly into a six-foot-wide stretch of lawn that separated the new bed from an existing garden under wild plum trees. Since there was little to define the space between the two gardens, we decided to cut new edges to form a lawn pathway between them. This path would, we hoped, pull the two gardens together and lead the eye as well as the stroller on to other parts of our garden.

Working with garden hoses, we experimented with a variety of shapes until we had the curves we wanted. (I sometimes outline a curve with lime, letting a handful run out of my hand as I walk along. If I get the line wrong, I simply rake the lime about, erasing the line, and start over.) The result is a graceful path 4 feet wide and some 30 feet long. To cut the edges, I simply pinned the hoses in place with my wire staples and, as before, followed this line with my half-moon edger to cut the turf (keeping the hose between me and the edger, and taking care not to slice the hose). Then I went back with my spade to undercut the turfs and remove them. The moment we finished pulling away the sod, the importance of crisp edges was reaffirmed. Each bed was more strongly defined, its shape standing out clearly, and the space between the beds had a purpose.

Around trees and shrubs

The immediate area around the trunk of a tree or shrub that's set in a lawn is a problem. Grass and weeds grow right up against the trunk. If you ride or push your lawn mower too close to the trunk you can skin off the bark. If you use a string trimmer next to the trunk, you either tear the bark or fail to trim all the grass. Or you spend a great deal of time on your hands and knees clipping the grass with shears.

Establishing an edge in the shape of a diamond around a tree or bush, with the length of the diamond running parallel to the direction you run your mower, is a good alternative. George

Cooper showed me a cardboard template he uses at Hidcote, and which he has seen used in many estates in England. They're easy to make.

Use a two-foot-wide, three-foot-long piece of sturdy cardboard (larger if you have trees more than 12 inches or so in diameter). Measure out eight inches from either side of the center of the cardboard, on the wide sides, and mark those points. This will form the width of the diamond. Now draw lines from those two points to the center of the other sides. Cut out that diamond shape, thus forming two pieces of cardboard which, when placed together, form a hole in the shape of the diamond. Place the template around the trunk of the tree. Stand on one side of the cardboard while you cut and lift out the sod within that half of the diamond. Then do the same for the other side. Now you'll be able to pass your lawn mower along the edge of the diamond without endangering the trunk of the shrub or tree. The price you have to pay for this ease is maintaining the edge with edging shears, weeding the now-open soil periodically.

MAINTAINING EDGES

Once established, lawn edges must be clipped regularly lest they become shaggy and lose their sharpness. Grass shears are the tool for this job, not the half-moon edger. The former is designed to cut blades of grass, the latter to slice through turf. Christopher Lloyd told me he won't allow the use of the half-moon to trim a lawn edge. "You have to cut something with the blade. It won't cut grass, so you cut just a little turf each time and the edge gets further and further from the bed, and weeds end up filling in the space." Each spring I do use my edger to spruce up an edge that has either fallen or grown—however slightly—into a bed over the winter.

To clip grass edges I use long-handled, vertical-action shears, an unlikely, oddly angled tool you may have seen in catalogs. I use these in large part because I prefer to do as much gardening as possible standing up rather than crawling around on all fours. Quality short-handled shears are perfectly good if you don't mind crawling as you clip. Long-handled string trimmers are not an option because their rotary blades are designed to cut parallel to the ground, and to trim an edge you need to cut perpendicular to the ground. A long-handled, vertical-action edging shear is a far more manageable tool once you get the hang of it.

It's worth the money to buy a good pair of edging shears rather than trying to save a few dollars on an inferior brand. There's nothing more frustrating than blades of grass binding between the blades of a pair of shears. The blades on quality shears hold their edge and continue to cut crisply for years. I've never had to sharpen a good pair. I also consider weight when purchasing edging shears. Those with tubular steel handles are considerably lighter than wooden-handled ones.

The English clip their edges once a week, and, if they do it on a warm, sunny day, the clippings are so small they are left in place to dry up and disappear. As much as I enjoy crisp edges, I simply don't have the time to keep my edges as tidy as that. Every two weeks or so, I clip them, pull the clippings into piles with a hoe, gather them in my wheelbarrow, and cart them to the compost heap.

There are two other methods to maintain edges—mechanical edgers and rolls of metal edging. I have found neither of these to be satisfactory. The only metal edging I've ever seen that's substantial enough to stay in place and do its job is four-inch-wide and one-eighth-inch-thick aluminum edging. This is a sturdy material held in place with solid pins, but it costs $1 a foot, a price that makes it unreasonable for most of us.

The other solution is to spend $200 or $300 for a motorized mechanical edger. Most of them have a cutting bar fashioned much like miniature rotary mower blades that can be set to spin vertically or horizontally. I cannot speak from experience, but I can imagine they are fraught with problems, mechanical and otherwise. Though professional groundskeepers no doubt find them helpful, I prefer a good pair of shears and the peaceful quiet they provide.

Good edges are good organizers, and I look to them for a lot of help now and again. A few years back, I realized one hot August day that I had a real mess of a bed and it was certainly the wrong time to transplant and rearrange. I put an edge on the bed, and afterwards I thought of a poem by Wallace Stevens, "Anecdote of the Jar." It's about perception and how simple objects—like a garden edge or a garden sculpture—can help us perceive order and organization in an apparently chaotic image.

> I placed a jar in Tennessee,
> And round it was, upon a hill.
> It made the slovenly wilderness
> Surround that hill.
> The wilderness rose up to it,
> And sprawled around, no longer wild. . .
> It took dominion everywhere.

A good edge, well maintained, will do the same and more.

22

GARDEN CLOTHS

Simple tools are best, and what could be simpler than a tarpaulin? A few years ago, while in the midst of restoring gardens and grounds for a client, I began to realize all the problems a simple garden cloth could solve, and how simplicity lends itself to versatility.

One morning I pulled into my client's driveway with a load of shrubs on my pickup truck. As I untied the 8-by-10-foot woven-polyethylene tarpaulin that I'd used to protect the shrubs from the wind, I was thinking about the planting I would do that day and the mess I would make on the lawn paths between the borders. I had brought plastic sheeting along, but I knew from experience that before long I'd tear it with my shovel and end up with soil and roots and peat scattered everywhere. Then it hit me. I could use the tarpaulin instead. It was of generous dimensions, was strong enough to be dragged along the ground when laden with soil, and it was tough—I wouldn't accidentally tear it with my shovel.

I spread the cloth so as to overlap the edge of the border and the lawn by a foot or so and started planting. An hour later the cloth was strewn with burlap wrapping, soil, stones, weeds, peat moss, prunings, and plant labels. I shoveled what soil I could back into the border and then pulled the cloth to the compost and refuse area, leaving behind a swatch of lawn that was as clean as when I began work.

Several days later I was weeding a deep perennial bed. Rather than use the wheelbarrow, a raised two-by-three-foot target enclosed on three sides, I spread out the 8-by-10-foot tarp. It didn't take me long to realize what good aim a wheelbarrow requires and how missing the target would break my concentration and waste my time. A tarp lying on the ground is tough to miss, and it holds a lot of weeds. After completing one section of border, I simply pulled the cloth along and loaded more weeds on. I then pulled up at the four corners of the cloth to gather the weeds in the center, took hold of two corners, and hauled the cloth off to the compost. (A cloth also makes negotiating down steps a snap.) To unload I just pulled the cloth up and rolled the weeds off. The only problem I've found is that I sometimes overload the cloth. When a wheelbarrow is too full you can see it's too full, but a cloth is only too full when you can't pull it along without straining yourself. If you're not paying attention you'll load it up well beyond that point.

Of course, there are many other uses for a garden cloth:

- to ease cleanup when a load of sand, gravel, mulch, or compost must be delivered onto a lawn or driveway.
- to cover materials such as sand, leaves, or loose compost when hauling them in a pickup truck.
- to collect and haul away leaves.
- to carry mulch or compost into a tightly planted shrub or flower border. With another person's help, you can then sift the mulch off the edge of the cloth and in between the tightly spaced plants.
- to catch twigs and branches when trimming a hedge or pruning a tree.
- to cover equipment that has to be left out overnight.
- to collect debris when dividing or transplanting perennials.
- to collect leaves or branches as they are spit from a shredder or chipper.

WHAT KIND OF CLOTH TO GET

Polyethylene garden cloths, either laminated or open-weave, with or without grommets, can be purchased in several colors, sizes, and weights from mailorder catalogs, garden centers, or discount houses. An 8-by-10-foot cloth is best for me, but you'll want to match cloth size to your strength and the size of your garden. I prefer an unlaminated cloth when working on a bank because it's not nearly as slippery as a laminated one, so weeds and trimmings stay where they land. Yet slippery, laminated cloths are easier to haul and unload. Since the cloths cost only between $8 and $15, I have one of each.

There are cloths made of other materials, but those create more problems than they solve. Burlap is difficult to haul and quite heavy when wet, and it wears out quickly. Canvas is not a good option for similar reasons. Clear plastic, as I've said, tears too easily, and it's so light that it becomes ruffled in a modest wind.

When you begin working with a garden cloth, you may come to the same conclusion I have reached: Once you combine simple tools with an open mind you realize that many tools are far more versatile than you thought.

23

WORK GLOVES

There is a tool or gadget designed to do nearly every gardening task imaginable, yet none of them would be worth much without the gardener's one essential tool: his hands. We gardeners abuse our hands at every turn, whether we're pruning rosebushes or blackberry canes, moving stones or setting bricks, planting or transplanting, or hauling and piling thorny brush. We work with sharp tools like shears, knives, handsaws, chain saws, and scythes. Our hands deserve protection.

I used to buy inexpensive cloth gloves by the dozen to protect my hands. They would last a week or two or, if I was rebuilding a stone wall, a morning. The gloves were so cheap I thought the practice made good economic sense. But cloth gloves offer little protection against a rose thorn, and with use they stretch all out of proportion to your hand and end up feeling loose and sloppy. I'd rather risk the odd cut or scrape than wear such gloves.

I've also used all types of leather gloves. Cowhide, pigskin, or buckskin gloves offer fine protection, but they make my hands feel clumsy. The thick leather forms bulky creases when I bend my fingers. Furthermore, once cowhide and pigskin get wet, they become stiff and uncomfortable. And because many gloves made from these hides are of rough suede, they readily absorb water and hold dirt, making them even stiffer when they've dried out.

So it was with great pleasure that I learned about goatskin gloves a few years ago. I was evaluating tools for David Tresemer, an expert on hand tools and at that time owner of a mailorder company. He suggested I try a pair of heavy-duty goatskin gloves his firm was selling. I did, and I've never looked back. The gloves are made by the Green Mountain Glove Company in Randolph, Vermont, where company owner Kurt Haupt has concluded that the finely grained, light-tan leather made of goatskin is more durable and at the same time more pliable and comfortable than any other. I agree.

GOATSKIN

There are three important differences between goatskin gloves and those made from pigskin, buckskin, or cowhide. (Hides, by the way, are from larger animals, skins from smaller.) First, goatskin is the most open-fibered of these leathers, making it the supplest and the warmest.

Second, because goatskin is so supple, Green Mountain Glove is able to use full-grained hides exclusively. What is a full-grained hide? Once rawhides have been tanned (that is, soaked in tannin and other chemicals), stretched, and dried, they can be split to make two or three hides of varying thickness and quality. The outer surface of the hide, the part that was the top layer of the animal's skin, is called full-grain leather. It's smooth and tough and resists abrasion. The splits, or suedes, are rough and less durable than grain leather, though they are generally very pliable.

The third difference is Green Mountain's workmanship. Its patterns are carefully designed to keep the gloves from binding at the knuckles and bunching up between the thumb and index finger. And the gloves are available with the seams tucked inside (as is done with most gloves) or left outside the glove fingers. Interior seams might be more attractive, but I've found that exterior seams are superior because the space for your fingers isn't partially filled with the seams. The seams-out design provides you with a better fit and more flexibility. Also, there are reinforcing welts at the tips of the three middle fingers and along the curve between the base of the thumb and forefinger. The patented thumb design provides further flexibility because there's no seam where the thumb attaches to the palm. Finally, Green Mountain's gloves are stitched with 100-percent nylon thread. The leather will wear out before this tough thread does, a blessing because I don't know what's worse than a perfectly good pair of gloves whose finger seams keep giving out.

Yet for all of this reinforcing and toughness, Green Mountain's is the softest, supplest, most comfortable heavy-duty work glove I've ever worn. And it's the most durable. I've used goatskin gloves for many heavy jobs, and the leather hasn't worn out nearly as quickly as cowhide. I've had one pair for more than a year, and they're still in good condition. That makes good economic sense, even though goatskin doesn't come cheap: a pair costs around $20.

SHEEPSKIN

Not all garden jobs require such sturdy gloves. My wife and I had been using a variety of lightweight cloth gloves over the years to prevent blisters caused by hours of repetitive work with one hand tool, whether it be hedge shears, a lawn rake, a spade, or a garden hoe. But we never found cloth to be very satisfactory. When we saw an advertisement in a mailorder catalog for a lightweight, creamy-white "goatskin" glove said to be rich in lanolin, we ordered a pair each. We knew sheep, not goats, produce lanolin, but we ignored the apparent contradiction. We've found that these soft, lanolin-rich gloves do prevent blisters. We've also found them to be remarkably supple and ideally suited to weeding, deadheading, grafting, thinning

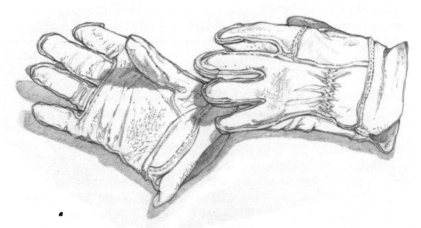

Goatskin leather imported from the Middle East is the secret of the supple and durable work gloves made by the Vermont Glove Company. Only recently did I discover these remarkable gloves, and learn what many other so-called "goatskin" gloves on the market are really made of.

seedlings, or other light work that requires less protection and more dexterity.

Recently, though, I discovered that these lightweight so-called goatskin gloves aren't made of goatskin at all. As you'd expect, they're made of sheepskin. Labels refer to the leather as "Napa goat" or as lanolin-enriched goatskin. One manufacturer told me that this mislabeling is industry-wide, and my inquiries didn't turn up a single manufacturer able to confirm that these distinctive creamy-white gloves are in fact goatskin.

I suspect that makers mislabel sheepskin to persuade customers that the gloves are tough. But sheepskin is not particularly tough. The soft, thin leather scuffs and tears easily against stones, bricks, or any rough surface and offers little protection against thorns and splinters. I've even found I have to make sure my fingernails are trimmed close. One of my thumbnails worked its way through a heavyweight leather even before the glove's fingertips had worn thin.

But for certain tasks sheepskin is perfect. I can untangle the delicate roots of a perennial I'm dividing, write out plant labels, tie my shoelaces, or pick up small objects without wasting time removing and then replacing my gloves. I've found, however, that soil sticks to the lanolin in sheepskin and tends to dry out the leather. But that same lanolin enables you to wash these gloves. The best way is to put the gloves on and wash them with a mild dishwashing liquid as if you were washing your hands. Then take them off and let them dry at room temperature. Don't wring them out or you'll force out much of the lanolin. After drying they're a bit stiff at first, but in a few minutes of use they regain most of their original suppleness. I did find, though, that with subsequent washings the gloves stiffened significantly.

There are two types of sheepskin gloves on the market, lightweight and heavyweight, neither of which is suitable for heavy-duty work. Both are made of grain leather that is naturally white (the lanolin rejects dyes). The difference in the two types seems to be in the quality of the leather. There is indeed a wide range of quality, both in leather and stitching, in lightweight sheepskin gloves, though they're all made of a distinctive, slightly crinkled and creased leather that's sometimes mottled light brown. The heavyweight gloves are made of a smoother leather that is sturdier and more abrasion-resistant but contains less lanolin. They retail for around $12.

Hands deserve gloves. We all know what it's like to work in the garden with a cut finger or a blistered palm. It's bothersome if not painful. We should choose gloves with the same care we bring to the choice of other tools.

24 🌼

RESTORING A
PERENNIAL GARDEN

Nature untended moves fast. Neglect a perennial garden for a month or two and common purslane spreads, lawn grasses creep in from the paths, and dandelions compete with primulas for the dominant yellow. Neglect a garden for a year or two and you've got a tangle of grass nearly smothering the few leggy lupines, daffodils, and coral-bell stems that manage to push their way through. Of all the arts, gardening is the most ephemeral.

The two pairs of 70-foot perennial beds that I began restoring for a client in Putney, Vermont, had been partially weeded but otherwise neglected for at least three years. Patches of open soil among the perennials were relatively free of weeds, but grasses and annual and perennial weeds, as well as lily of the valley and wild violets had invaded peony crowns and iris drifts, moss phlox and daylilies, hollyhocks and hardy geraniums. No organic matter had been added to the soil in years. It was exhausted and dry. Daylily clumps and bearded-iris rhizomes were so crowded they were forcing themselves out of the ground. Siberian iris formed nearly impenetrable four- to five-foot-wide mats of roots, each mat dead at the center.

These had once been fine borders, deserving of restoration, not uprooting. Frederick dePuyster Townsend, an occasional collaborator of the Olmsted Brothers design firm, designed the garden at Faraway Farm for his daughter in the early 1940s. She saw to the careful upkeep of the gardens until her death in 1980, after which her caretaker kept them weeded as best he could until the property was sold in 1983. In April 1984 the new owners hired me to restore them.

Working one or two days a week now and again during two growing seasons, following a restoration schedule that respected the idiosyncrasies of the plants and the appropriate times for dividing them, I brought the weeds under control and rebuilt the soil. Divisions of perennials were completed, and new planting designs took on a coherence. The restoration of a garden is hard work and it takes time, but for all that, the process and the product are full of satisfaction.

UNDERSTANDING THE CONTEXT

Before restoring a garden, I take a look at it from several vantage points and try to understand its context and overall structure. It was from the barnyard to the west of and at the top of the garden that I was able to discern Townsend's organizing principle. It proved to be a discovery rich in implications for restoration.

The 90-by-120-foot rectangular garden is enclosed by stone walls. It is aligned on an east-west axis, the focal point being Mount Monadnock, some 40 miles east across the Connecticut River Valley. Two arborvitae at the bottom, or east end of the garden frame the view and emphasize that central axis. On either side of a central, sunken lawn, Townsend aligned two pairs of 70-foot-long beds parallel with this major axis—on the north side, two full-sun borders bisected by a straight lawn path, on the south, two shade beds separated by a curving lawn path.

The discovery of the central axis enabled me to understand the organizing principle the designer apparently had in mind: two pairs of beds with opposite qualities. The south pair featured shade, a curving path, and an informal planting scheme. The north pair had full sun, a straight path, and a more formal planting scheme.

To get a different view, I walked up into the field to the south of the garden and looked down through a row of three towering apple trees that shaded the southern pair of borders. From that vantage point it was clear that the lower limbs should be pruned off to let in more air and light. I would do that the following winter when the trees were dormant.

I then went to the north of the garden and into the 200-year-

old farmhouse that sits 100 feet across the lawn from the garden. Looking out of the downstairs window, I realized how
important tall flowers in the borders would be: from their
kitchen, dining room, or living room the owners should see
color over the stone wall enclosing the beds and lawn.

After gaining an appreciation of the importance Townsend
had placed on pattern and axis, I studied the borders and the
paths between them, starting with the shade beds. From the
clues provided by ground contours and edges, I could see that
the original path was an elongated S-curve. What was left of it
was an unsatisfying, free-form grass path that over the years
had worked its way well into the beds. This pair of borders
threw yellow, blue, and purple flowers, a satisfying combination, but the blue from an overabundance of columbine was
overwhelming the other colors. Only one clump of yellow
primula survived, the forsythia was dying back, and the yellow
azaleas needed pruning. The purple Siberian iris was so overcrowded it could barely produce flowers.

In the full-sun borders were the remnants of a far more
formal planting scheme than that which Townsend had used in
the shade beds. Here he had planted five six- to eight-foot
drifts of bearded iris at regular intervals along the length of
both beds. Between those drifts he had planted peonies and
phlox at equally regular intervals. These three plants formed
the backbone of his design. Interspersed were either specimen
plants such as fraxinella or hybrid lilies, for accent, or clumps of
plants—daylilies, perennial geraniums, hollyhocks, Oriental
poppies, and a few columbines from across the way.

It was clear this more formal planting scheme had gone
awry. Several clumps of phlox, as well as several peony
crowns, had either died or been removed. Many of the
bearded-iris clumps had begun to die back in the center because of overcrowding. Moss phlox was far beyond its original
limits and was creeping around peony and phlox crowns.

WEEDING AND EDGING

With some understanding of the past, and with a better understanding of the parts as they related to the whole, I began the
physical work. I first went through the beds and uprooted

weeds that were about to go to seed. Dandelions and goose grass (*Eleusine indica*) went first, while stoloniferous quack grass (*Agropyron repens*) and annual weeds not yet gone to seed went next. Herein lies a principle of garden restoration: The present relates intimately to the future. Do what you can to reduce the number of weed seeds released into the garden now, and you'll have fewer problems later. I should add that in this case, with so many plants, I didn't restore the garden by uprooting all the perennials, pulling all the weeds, and starting over, the approach I use in small gardens. Each perennial requires different soil conditions, and each has its own appropriate time to be divided. But more of this later.

My next task is always to clean up the edges. At Faraway Farm I began by stretching white cord along the edge between the path and the full-sun perennial beds. Then, using a straight-nosed spade, I cut the sod, using the cord as a guide. I collected the strips of sod in a cart and hauled the load to the lawn to fill in bare spots. Because each part of a garden relates to the whole, I never throw anything on the compost heap until I have considered its use in other parts of the garden.

WAYS TO SMOTHER WEEDS

There are other simple solutions you can use, if grass and weeds have taken firm hold of a perennial bed right to its very center. First, dig up any perennials you want to save, preferably in the spring. Pull weed and grass roots from the root systems, cut off what growth on the perennials appears leggy and broken, and set them in a nursery bed you've prepared beforehand. The chances are that the plants, as battered as they might appear, will survive if you transplant them with care and keep them watered and mulched. Then get out the rotary lawn mower or a scythe and cut the grass and weeds in the garden down to ground level.

The problem now is to eradicate the grass and weed roots. Herbicides are one solution, but they create more problems than their use justifies. There are chemical residues to consider, and you still have the sod to contend with. Here is a simpler solution.

If the area is of manageable size, first outline the edges with white cord and cut the outer perimeter with a straight-nosed spade. Then dig up the sod with a shovel, being sure to get up as many pieces of broken grass roots as possible, as they will readily take hold the minute you turn your back.

There is an even simpler solution, however: smother the roots. This can be done in two ways. If you want to create a new perennial bed immediately, enclose the area with a wooden or stone retaining wall at least eight inches high, and fill the enclosure with enriched topsoil. The grass roots below will die off and eventually decompose, thus providing organic matter. This garden can be planted immediately.

The fourth option takes a year, very little work, and results in a garden at ground level. Spread a sheet of heavy-gauge black plastic over what will be the garden. Weigh the plastic down with flat rocks and spread two or three inches of wood chips or bark mulch on top of the plastic so as to hide it from view and keep it flat on the ground. Or you can cover the entire surface of the proposed garden with old planks. Return in a year. Take up the mulch and plastic, or the woodpile, and you will find that the root systems of virtually all the plants underneath have died, if not decomposed. The soil can then be turned with a rotary tiller or a shovel, and what roots remain can be pulled from the broken soil. Add generous amounts of compost and peat moss to refurbish the soil, and you have a new perennial bed ready to plant.

REMOVING AND TRANSPLANTING

At Faraway Farm, once the initial weeding was completed and the edges delineated, I turned my attention to sections of the garden that had been overrun by freely seeding perennials like columbine and hollyhock. Such a problem can be turned into a solution by trading seedlings and, later, divisions of any number of abundant plants with fellow gardeners. In doing so you introduce new plants into the garden without having to spend money, and you can offer friends new plants for their gardens.

Over time, some perennials invade through profligate seeding, while others creep along the surface, and it was these creepers that I dealt with next. *Phlox stolonifera* had crept into the bearded iris, and *Phlox paniculata* had spread right up to the edge of several peony crowns. I uprooted both species of phlox back to a healthy distance from other perennials, then transplanted those divisions into a 20-by-30-foot nursery-*cum*-storage area I had dug in a vegetable garden behind the barn. Such a nursery is a must in the early stages of any restoration project because a neglected garden is invariably overcrowded. The extra divisions become the backups. Furthermore, you need to see what colors you are working with before incorporating them into the borders. In the case of *Phlox paniculata*, I wouldn't know their colors until late August.

Selectively removing those extra plants that result from seeding or creeping creates spaces in the garden for new divisions and introductions. Once I had transplanted unwanted columbines, I took several divisions of Siberian iris and planted them in drifts against the background of the stone wall in the moist shade garden. I also divided and transplanted the one clump of yellow primula so as to begin the process of restoring the yellow-blue-purple balance in that bed. I made a note that I would need to purchase more yellow primulas. I waited until after bloom to take divisions of the daylilies because I wanted to be sure what colors I was working with.

While walking to and from the garden during those early days of work, I was always on the lookout for what so often accompanies a neglected perennial bed—a neglected compost pile. I've found them under tangles of stinging nettle and brambles, at the bases of stone retaining walls, and near collapsed brick or cinder-block enclosures at the edge of the woods. At Faraway Farm I found it by the barn, and it was a mother lode. The mound was 3 feet high, 20 feet in diameter, and covered with quack grass and nettles. After a morning's work, my helper and I uncovered enough decomposed cow manure to enrich the soil in all four beds.

Because it was then early June and many perennials were in bloom, I took the opportunity to label those that I would later want to divide and increase. Labeling is something I do throughout the first season of any restoration project; otherwise, with the many divisions, confusion is inevitable. In one broad drift of nondescript yellow bearded iris, for example, I discovered a handsome clump of the purple-and-white cultivar 'Stepping Out'. I marked each flower stalk in that clump so that

A step-by-step process incorporates the techniques and the philosophy behind the work necessary to restore a neglected perennial bed. The example is the garden at Faraway Farm in Putney, Vermont, but the principles are universal.

three weeks later, when it came time to restore the bearded-iris beds, we would be able to find and increase 'Stepping Out' while reducing the number of yellow iris.

To ensure blooms the following year, I divide bearded iris shortly after they have bloomed but before the new feeder rootlets begin to develop in early August. By waiting until that optimum time for lifting and dividing the rhizomes, I can combine several processes in one operation: I lift the rhizomes, uproot the quack grass, rebuild the soil with compost, increase special rhizomes, and reduce the number of less desirable ones.

The irises are a good example of my methods. I said earlier that I restore each section of the garden at the appropriate time for dividing perennials in that section. Chrysanthemums, bee balm, evening primrose, and other stoloniferous plants are divided in early spring; Siberian iris and phlox when their shoots are two or three inches high; daylilies just after they have bloomed; peony plantings in early September. And of course throughout the entire growing season I keep the edges maintained and the weeds from going to seed.

In lifting and dividing so many plants, one must make amends for the partial destruction of their root systems. Because the foliage of a plant grows in proportion to its root system, and because lifting and dividing invariably damage the roots, it is important to trim the foliage back in proportion to the damage done to the root system. Before resettling the bearded-iris rhizomes I cut off the top six or eight inches of the leaves. Otherwise they would have continued to transpire at the same rate as before their roots were damaged, and the plants would have dehydrated themselves.

MAINTAINING VIGILANCE

Back to weeds. The soil in any neglected garden has an abundance of weed seeds, and it takes constant vigilance to keep them from becoming mature, seed-bearing plants. Grasses also are persistent. In digging up quack-grass roots, you must pick every last section of root out of the soil. Yet no matter how careful you are, invariably you miss small pieces. A week or two later little green blades of grass poke through, just when you're beginning to relax and think that you've permanently reclaimed your garden. Not so. Maintain vigilance especially during the first year and you'll be rewarded. Fail, and the grass and weeds will grow with renewed vigor; they respond to compost just as perennials do.

It's also important, in the midst of all this seeding, dividing, and snipping of dead flower heads, to note what I did not do.

Certain perennials should not be moved. Mature hollyhocks and fraxinella, for example, have deep and brittle taproots, which preclude successful transplanting, so I left them right where they were and dug in compost around them. But I didn't enrich the soil around the peonies with the manure compost for fear that it carried *Botrytis* fungi; leaf mold was safer. I also didn't add annuals to the garden. I left many bare spots so that there would be plenty of room for divisions.

In late September I went back to the garden for one final weeding. I also cut back the hollyhocks, phlox, and peonies and burned the tops to destroy insect eggs that might have been laid on the leaves. Here again it's important to note what I didn't do. I didn't cut back the bearded-iris leaves to ground level. They are better left to flop over so that when it rains the water doesn't run down the inside of the severed stems, carrying rot or fungi into the rhizomes. The following spring is time enough to clean up the iris beds.

WINTER PLANNING

In the quiet of winter I considered what perennials to introduce in the newly restored garden in the spring. Several questions helped me find good answers. What new colors or textures would complement those in the existing garden? Which new cultivars would extend the blooming season of particular species? What plants could be added to help unify the design? We needed whites, pinks, and light reds to enliven the dominant deep blue of the columbines in the shade bed, so I ordered 15 *Primula japonica*, the candelabra primula. I also ordered *Phlox divaricata*, another late-spring bloomer, to soften the blues already in the bed. To add further texture and foliage color to the shade bed, I ordered five thalictrums, several *Hosta sieboldiana* 'Elegans', and several clumps of baptisia. To introduce a deep red that could be seen from the house, I ordered several clumps of the native bee balm (*Monarda didyma*) and stippled them throughout the bed.

For more color in the adjoining semishade bed, I ordered five clumps each of *Hemerocallis* 'Elizabeth' and 'Gold Dust', both of which are extra-early daylilies that would extend the blooming season and add yellow. To increase the interplay of texture in that same bed, I selected 12 mature clumps of a light pink dianthus with its soft silver-gray foliage to act as a foil for the daylily leaves and to add color to that bed in June.

I wanted white phlox in the sun borders to reestablish the regular spacing of those clumps, so I ordered several *P. decussata* 'Mt. Fuji'. Peonies were needed to reestablish their regular spacing, to add new and complementary colors, and to extend the bloom. I ordered two late-blooming herbaceous peonies, the cherry-rose hybrid 'Cytherea' and 'Lovely Rose'.

With spring's arrival, I weeded assiduously once again, set out the new perennials, and began the season-long process of making the many necessary divisions of phlox, Siberian iris, and those daylilies I hadn't gotten to the previous summer. I used those divisions to fill in gaps and to carry on Townsend's planting patterns.

Throughout the restoration of any garden, I keep certain principles in mind. First, unless my clients ask me to be one, I am not a purist. I do not rigidly hold to the dictums implied by my predecessors in the garden. As Russell Page put it, "I see little sense in being too much a purist. . . . To follow slavishly even the best models may well make your garden look too laboured and too sententious." So many improved cultivars have been introduced since Townsend designed and planted the garden at Faraway Farm that it would be irresponsible of me to turn my back on those advancements in color, growth habit, and variety. Having said that, I try to save what is good about the original garden: the designs and patterns, the color schemes and plant choices, the architectural elements. Many of these have ripened over time, and time lends a certainty, a maturity, and an equanimity to a garden that are difficult if not impossible to replace.

25

ESPALIERS

Pruning, the essence of fruit-tree espaliers (pronounced ess-PAL-yers), takes a stout heart. We must go to the apple or pear tree, sharp shears in hand, and make life-or-death decisions. Snip, and the inferior branch is banished to the burn pile. We must accept that there are better twigs, better fruiting spurs, and that they must be allowed to live out their superior lives.

Pruning doesn't come easy to us Americans; perhaps this, in part, explains why the espaliered fruit tree has never been widely accepted here. "Live free or die" declares the New Hampshire license plate. Let the apple or pear trees in the backyard grow as they will. Let there be freedom, dignity for all, equality among all branches. And that way, there will be no badly pruned fruit trees standing there all year long displaying the results of our ignorance.

Europeans don't have the same attitude toward pruning. This, I suspect, is because they must impose a greater degree of order on unruly nature than Americans. Europeans don't have abundant land, and they have had to develop myriad skills in order to make the very best of what land they do have. Severe pruning is a skill you must have, and exercise, if you want to raise bountiful crops of fruit on very little land.

On the summer day when John Baldwin and his father, Jack, showed me the espaliered 'Pit Maston Duchess' pear that grows on the south wall of John's farmhouse in Gloucestershire, England, I was struck by how much the American gardener could learn from that tree and all it represents. The 80-year-old espalier grows from a narrow strip of grass between the wall and the driveway. Over the decades it has yielded hundreds of bushels of fruit, yet it occupies no more than a few square feet of soil surface. It reflects a mature harmony between the practical and the beautiful, for the espalier is, above all, an attractive, yet intensive, cropping system that results from careful pruning.

As the finite amount of land and its increasing cost force us to rethink our attitudes about land use, we realize that we must explore how best to use every available plot of soil in our gardens to create attractive, yet practical, results. While keeping in mind the best modern advancements in horticulture, the direction in which we might turn for "new" standards is the Old World. French intensive gardening is one example. The espaliered fruit tree is another.

The espalier combines the old with the new in a most graceful way. The best modern cultivars can be raised on clonal, semidwarfing rootstock following traditional European planting and pruning methods. In so doing, we can raise abundant crops of apples or pears in a way that is aesthetically pleasing and that requires no more space than a two-foot strip running along the south side of a garage, a site we might not have considered suitable for raising fruit trees.

There are several other reasons to consider planting espaliered apple and pear trees. The trained tree growing on semidwarfing rootstock yields significant amounts of fruit as early as its third or fourth year, whereas the standard tree takes six or seven years to yield abundantly. The yield per square foot of garden space from espaliers is much higher than that of either the standard-shaped semidwarfs or standard-size trees.

Because the heights of most espaliers are kept at eye level or below, the trees can be managed with ease. Pruning, thinning, spraying, and harvesting can all be done without ladders. And because the espalier is typically sited in the main part of the garden, one takes more notice of it, pruning the wood and thinning the fruits with greater care. This results in annual rather than biennial fruiting; the tree is strong enough to produce both this year's fruit and next year's buds simultaneously.

A NEW SKILL

But all these advantages don't come easily. The trees must be chosen with care; a sturdy and permanent wire-support system must be put in place and maintained; above all, an exacting and regular late-winter and summer pruning and training program must be followed to maintain plentiful cropping on shapely trees. You must be committed to learning a new skill.

It's a skill that, though new to you, dates back at least 400 years. Many authorities credit Claude Mollet, head gardener at Fontainebleau for Henry III and Henry IV, with developing the espaliered fruit tree. He knew that planting trees against a south-facing stone or brick wall would result in the fruit ripening with more speed, color, and flavor. If those trees were severely pruned, more sunlight would strike the wall, thus enabling it to absorb and reflect more heat than would a leafier tree. Pruning the trees severely according to a carefully devised method, Mollet encouraged the formation of more fruiting spurs and fewer leaves. Furthermore, he saw that planting espaliers close to one another caused them to grow less vigorously and thus produce more fruit and fewer leaves than trees planted further apart.

Espalier, used as both a noun and a verb, is a French word that's probably derived from the Italian *spalliera*, meaning something against which to rest the shoulder. Both the word and the method came from France to England in the seventeenth century and referred originally to the trellis against which the plant was trained. There is some confusion today as to just what the term means. The Brooklyn Botanic Garden pamphlet on trained plants says, "The widest possible meaning of espalier today might be 'any flattened tree, shrub, or vine trained in any way.' " That appears to be the American definition. The modern English and French meaning is a bit more exacting, making a distinction between cordons, fan-training, and espaliers. Some English gardening books refer to cordons—three- to four-foot-long single-stems that are trained vertically or at a 45-degree angle to wires—as a category separate from espaliers. Others say the cordon is a kind of espalier. Fan-training is a method of training fruit trees, such as the peach and nectarine, that bear only on new wood. The branches are literally trained in a fan shape. But the definition really can't be that strict, because there are fan-trained apple trees at the Royal Horticultural Society gardens at Wisley, in Surrey, England.

My definition of espalier is the one used by the older professional English gardeners, like George Cooper at Hidcote

Manor, and as such it is a rather narrow definition: An espalier is an apple or pear tree trained in two dimensions, standing in the open or against a wall, the pruning method of which follows certain traditional patterns.

Espaliers thus defined divide into three basic patterns: vertically or horizontally trained branches, or variations on the two. The simplest vertical is the single-stem cordon, from which can be developed the single-, double-, or triple-U forms. Also within this family are the four- and six-armed Palmette Verriers, the latter considered the most elegant of all espaliers. The basic horizontal is one to six tiers of branches trained horizontally to the right and left of the trunk. Of the variations, the Belgian Fence is one of the simplest and most attractive.

Two options

If you would like to plant pear or apple espaliers, you have two options. The first, by far the easier (but more expensive) is to purchase already-trained trees from an expert. Henry P. Leuthardt Nurseries in New York is one of the few nurseries in this country that specialize in espaliers. It has done so for generations, both on Long Island and, before that, in private gardens in Switzerland.

Write to Leuthardt (Montauk Highway, East Moriches, NY 11940) for his catalog, and, if you send a dollar along, he will send you his brochure on how to select, plant, and prune espaliers. He offers several cultivars of pear and apple trees that are trained in traditional patterns. They're an absolute marvel to receive by parcel post.

A recent catalog listed a six-armed Palmette Verrier, a tree Henry Leuthardt had worked on for perhaps seven years. Costing $100 to $125, the tree was five and a half feet tall and just as wide and would yield about a bushel of fruit per year. At the other extreme, a single vertical cordon of the same height cost only $11. Leuthardt will also give you advice on hardiness, cross-pollination, planting, siting, and wire suspension systems.

The other option is to purchase one-year-old "clean-stemmed maidens," as they are called in England, a term much preferable to the American term, "whip." You can buy these young, unbranched trees from Leuthardt, your nurseryman, or many mailorder houses. You can then train the tree.

Before purchasing any trees, be certain that the cultivar you choose has been grafted onto dwarfing or semidwarfing rootstock. Espaliers on standard root systems become unmanageable. Most nurserymen who grow trained trees graft known cultivars onto dwarfing rootstock. They use basically three different kinds: Malling 26, Malling 7A, and MM-106, all of which were developed in England.

Malling 26 rootstock dwarfs to about 50 percent of standard size. It doesn't do well in slowly draining soils. Also, if you are planting in Zone 4 or north, don't use it, as the stock is only medium hardy. The Malling 7A rootstock dwarfs to about 60 percent of standard size. It's the most widely planted semidwarfing stock and is more sturdy than Malling 26. It's hardy to Zone 4 and transplants well. If you plant it in light, sandy soil, add some humus at planting time, because it doesn't do as well in quickly draining soils. The MM-106 rootstock dwarfs to about 70 percent. It's particularly suited to spur-type trees such as 'McIntosh' and is equal to the Malling 7A in hardiness.

For apple espaliers in Zone 3 or north, you might try the recently developed Ottawa rootstocks developed by the Canadian government. According to Lewis Hill, professional orchardist from northern Vermont and author of *Successful Cold Climate Gardening*, their No. 3 appears to be the best. You should also ask your nurseryman which apple cultivars are hardy in Zone 3 and north. Many of the new ones aren't. Lewis Hill recommends 'Astrachan', 'Blue Permain', 'Connell', 'Fameuse', 'Lodi', or 'Wealthy'. Hill cautions people in Zone 3 and north that espaliers are fairly unproductive. "But then," he adds, "with careful pruning they might just work."

Cultivar and rootstock choices for pear espaliers are not nearly as complicated. Pear trees are dwarfed with quince rootstock. Because of this, dwarfed pear trees will not withstand sustained temperatures of minus 15 degrees Fahrenheit or colder. Even in northern Massachusetts, which is about the limit for dwarf pears in the Northeast, Leuthardt recommends

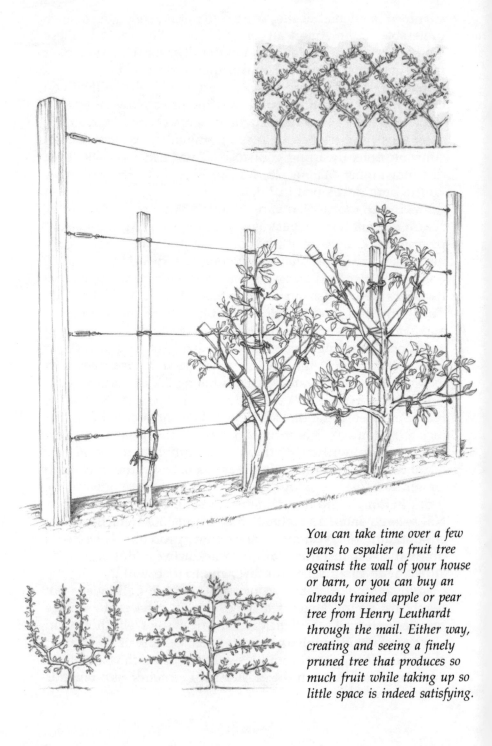

You can take time over a few years to espalier a fruit tree against the wall of your house or barn, or you can buy an already trained apple or pear tree from Henry Leuthardt through the mail. Either way, creating and seeing a finely pruned tree that produces so much fruit while taking up so little space is indeed satisfying.

planting on the south side of the house to mitigate the effects of cold.

POLLINATION AND SITING

Once you've decided on rootstock, you must consider the pollination requirements of your trees. Choose at least two pear trees or two apple trees that bloom at about the same time. Most apples must be cross-pollinated. All pears are self-sterile and must be cross-pollinated.

The problem of pollination is compounded if you plant espaliers next to a house or high stone or brick wall. Because warmth from the sun will collect in or be reflected by the wall, an espalier grown next to that wall will bloom earlier than a fruit tree planted in the open. Cross-pollination between the two might not be possible. To avoid this, plant at least two espaliers next to one another.

In the event that you can plant only one espalier, as John Baldwin's forebears did, there's a simple trick to encourage cross-pollination. When your espalier is in full bloom, snip branches from another pear or apple cultivar that's also in full bloom. Place those branches in a bucket of water and hang it in or very near your espalier. With luck, the bees will do the rest.

The next consideration is where to plant your tree. If you want an espalier solely for ornamental purposes, you can plant it virtually anywhere. But if you want trees that will bear fruit, plant them where they'll get at least six hours of sun. Full sun is preferable. You might use espaliers to separate the vegetable garden from the lawn. Or one might be planted as a feature on a terrace or patio. The attractive Belgian Fence, which requires a minimum of five trees to create the characteristic diamond shapes, can be used to form the backdrop for a sitting area.

If you do plant against a wall, choose one that faces southeast to southwest. If the wall is light colored, such as a white clapboard house, Leuthardt cautions you to keep the espalier anywhere from 12 to 18 inches away from the wall. During the dormant period, sunlight reflected from the wall could thaw the wood. At night it would refreeze, cracking the bark. If the wall is darker, keep the tree at least six inches out from the wall.

Whether you're planting against a wall or in the open, a horizontal wire support system is essential. At this point, I feel a bit like Eleanor Perenyi as she concluded the entry on asparagus in her book, *Green Thoughts*: "Whenever I write about gardening, I am struck by the amount of physical labor I seem to be describing. On paper it sounds overwhelming—but that is in the nature of written directions. The reality is not so onerous."

If you plan to purchase previously trained trees, wait until they arrive before setting up your suspension system. Plant the tree and then suspend your wires to accommodate the shape of the tree. If you plan to train your own, you can set the suspension wires beforehand. Leuthardt suggests the following method for suspending espaliers against a wall. First, drill a pair of one-inch-deep holes in your wall, 10 feet apart and 12 to 18 inches above the ground. Set one-inch lead anchors in the holes and then screw threaded eyebolts tightly into the anchors so they're secure enough to take the tension of taut wires. If you're training your espaliers against a light-colored wall, use longer eyebolts so the tree will be at least a foot away from the wall. Then drill holes at one-foot intervals above the bottommost ones, depending on the number of tiers you envision for your tree.

Once the eyebolts are securely in place, affix wires horizontally between the pairs of eyebolts. Use galvanized size 14 wire for larger espaliers, plastic or vinyl-coated wire for smaller espaliers. Vertical espaliers don't need vertical wires. Simply wire one-quarter- to one-half-inch bamboo stakes or wooden lath to the horizontal wires wherever support is needed. Saw the lath in half lengthwise so they're about three-quarter-inch wide. These wooden supports are especially attractive with the Belgian Fence or other intricate patterns, because they help define the shapes and symmetry in the early years, when the design isn't clearly delineated.

Wires for trees planted in the open should be strung between wooden posts set 10 to 12 feet apart. Besides being more attractive than metal, wood doesn't heat up on hot summer days the way metal does. For six-foot-high espaliers, use eight- or nine-foot-long black locust or cedar posts if you can—these woods are long lasting. Other wood must be treated with a wood preservative such as copper naphthenate, which is nontoxic to plants.

Set the posts two or three feet into the ground and then brace them against the pull of the wires with a diagonal stay post. Place the bases of the stay posts against a brick or large, flat stone and set the top of the stay post into a notch near the top of each end post. The wires should be placed at one-foot intervals up the post and connected to three-inch turnbuckles so they can be drawn taut. Properly set horizontal wires are essential to well-trained espaliers.

Ties are another consideration. Avoid those with wire cores, as they can cut into the tender bark. Jute cord, raffia, or ser-rated slip-on ties are good. Whatever material you choose, be sure it doesn't restrict the growth of the branches.

SOIL PREPARATION

A week or two before your trees arrive, dig a hole that's at least two feet square, to aerate and loosen the soil. As you dig, separate the topsoil from the subsoil. Once the hole is dug, line the bottom with topsoil, throw in two handfuls of lime, and then mix the two together. If the soil is dry, as is often the case at the base of masonry walls, mix in compost or leafmold to help retain moisture. Next, place the roots on the mixture so that the graft, which you'll find near the base of the trunk, is at least two inches above ground level. If you cover that graft with soil, roots will eventually sprout from the wood above it, thus bypassing the dwarfing habit of the rootstock. Your tree will eventually revert to standard size.

As you add additional topsoil, jiggle the tree up and down a bit so that all the air pockets around the roots fill with soil. When the roots are covered, tamp lightly and water heavily. After 10 minutes or so, add all the remaining soil and tamp it down with the heel of your foot and water heavily again. To keep espaliers within bounds, and to prevent unnecessary pruning, do not use fertilizer in or on the soil.

If you're planting espaliers against a masonry wall that has a footing, you'll have to bend the roots outward, with care, so that they're directed away from it. Apple and pear trees will not penetrate through the cracks in the foundation wall, nor will lime from the cement adversely affect the tree. In fact, pears thrive in soil with a pH of up to 8.0, apples in soil that is 6.0.

After planting, water heavily at least once a week and mulch with three inches of hay or straw until the trees are well established. Mulch will also help keep the grass and weeds from returning to the soil, where they'll compete with the tree's feeder rootlets.

Each fall enclose the trunks of your espaliers in a rodent-proof guard that reaches up to the depth of the snow. This will prevent the trees from being girdled during the winter by hungry animals living beneath the snow.

The planting distance between trees is determined by how they will be pruned. Horizontals are typically 10 feet apart. Use your own sense of proportion to determine the planting distance for other patterns.

THE PRUNING PROGRAM

Now comes the subtle, discerning work of training the clean-stemmed maiden. Here begins a pruning program that will call upon you to be strong of heart. Be determined. You'll be rewarded with good fruit, a handsome tree, and a great deal of satisfaction, part of which will come from a sense of kinship with generations of European gardeners.

Let's assume that you'll begin by creating a simple, horizontally trained espalier. Your young tree will probably be about four feet high. Plant it in front of and just touching the wires. Now prepare to banish up to two-thirds of your tree to the rubbish heap. Cut the stem to a bud two inches above the first wire in such a way that you have one bud to the right, one bud to the left, and one that will form the upright.

Over the next few weeks, keep an eye on your tree. If any of the three buds do not "break"—that is, begin to grow—make a minute, half-inch incision with a razor blade or sharp pocketknife just above that bud. That cut will form a kind of dam that will send more sap into the bud. It's not uncommon for the lower of the three buds to lag behind the others, so if you see this happening, make the incision. You should also rub out any buds other than the three, which will form the side and upright shoots.

By mid June in most areas of the country, those three buds will have grown into one-foot-long shoots. Fasten bamboo canes at a 45-degree angle from the horizontal support near the base of the two side shoots out and up to the second wire. Tie the flexible shoots of new growth to the canes. Then fasten a third bamboo cane from the wire near the base of the upright shoot directly upward to the second wire. Tie the shoot to it.

If you find that one side shoot is growing significantly faster than the other, you can regulate its growth, to a degree. Lowering the cane to a more acute angle will slow the growth of that shoot by impeding the flow of sap. Raising the angle will encourage growth by easing the flow.

Around late August, the two side shoots should be untied from the bamboo canes and tied firmly to the bottom wire. Be careful not to break the shoot off, but at the same time get the whole of the shoot as horizontal as possible.

In late winter, a few weeks before sap begins to flow, give your espalier another pruning. The upright should be cut back to about two inches above the second wire. Again you'll be looking for three buds, one to form the future upright and two that will form the right and left arms of your second tier.

There is some disagreement as to whether the horizontals should be pruned back or allowed to grow until they reach their desired length. Haden Williams, the fruit foreman at Wisley, teaches his trainees to cut back the horizontal shoots to insure strong new growth and good spur development on the older growth. The purist approach is to cut back strong leaders by one half and weak ones by more than half. Be sure to cut at least one-quarter inch beyond a strong, uppermost bud, as that will form the new extending growth.

If you don't want to be quite such a purist, simply allow the horizontal shoots to grow to their desired length and then shear off the tips. If more than one shoot arises as it grows toward its eventual length, leave the straightest and remove the others. Fruiting spurs will not develop as quickly as they would following the other method, but the difference will be minimal.

Once your upright has given rise to one-foot-long shoots,

around mid June, you begin the process of the previous June: tying the side shoots at 45-degree angles, increasing or decreasing the angle if need be, and so forth. Each year you follow this process to add on a new tier, so that by the end of the fifth year you have a five-tiered espalier.

When the horizontally trained espalier has reached its desired height, wait until the late-winter pruning to halt its upward growth. Cut the leading shoot so that you leave a bud going to the left and one to the right. Rub out any other buds that develop in an upward direction on that central stem. This will stop any further growth of the trunk.

All the same principles operate for shaping other traditional espaliers. If you want to train your trees into some of the more complex shapes, it would be best to find a complete book on this. Time-Life's *Pruning and Grafting* is particularly good.

MAKING IT FRUIT

Shaping an espalier is one thing; making it fruit is another. Most pear and apple trees produce fruit on what are called spurs. A fruiting spur is a contorted, stout twig about six inches long. At the tip of the spurs you'll see the swollen, round flower bud of the apple or the more slender, pointed, yet swollen flower bud of the pear. Each will be surrounded by small leaf buds.

The pruning method for established espaliers, known as the modified Lorette system, is named after Louis Lorette, a distinguished orchardist from France. The method is designed to encourage the formation of fruiting buds on pear and apple trees. It's not used commercially, because it's so time consuming.

The modified Lorette system entails frequent summer pruning and the heading back of leaders in very early spring, before the sap begins to flow. This causes fruit to develop along all the branches, unlike the standard tree, on which fruit develops only on the ends of the limbs.

Leuthardt recommends doing your summer pruning on the fifteenth of June, July, and August. On or around June 15 of the second and subsequent years after planting, you'll see that the first flush of growth has resulted in new upward growth from the branches. These are called laterals. They have arisen not only from the spurs but also from the main limb. These immature laterals have wispy green stems with leaves spaced much farther apart than those of the more mature spurs. Find the basal clump of leaves of each new lateral. Count up three leaves from that and make a slanting cut one-quarter inch above that third leaf.

On the lower branches of your maturing espalier, you'll find more mature laterals growing from both the spurs and the limbs themselves. Find the basal leaves of the new growth. Count up one leaf from that and make a slanting cut just above it.

If all this sounds a bit too complicated, simply do the following and call it a modified modified Lorette system. On the fifteenth of June, July, and August, cut every lateral back to four to six inches from the main arms. You will not be far off the mark. You may also find that, as the tree gets older, spurs begin to crowd one another. If so, thin them out to three to five inches apart.

If any fruits begin to form in the second or even third year, pull them off. Let the full energy of the tree go into root formation. In the fourth and subsequent years, when fruits do develop, thin them to six inches apart in every direction. Only in this way will you get large pears and apples. When harvesting the fruit, twist the apple or pear as you lift upward. Do this gently, as the fruiting spurs are brittle. Espaliered fruit trees require the same applications of fungicide and pesticide as other fruit trees. If your espalier is against a wall, use a sheet of plastic or cardboard to protect the wall from being discolored by the sprays.

The espalier is indeed complex. There's no getting around that fact. But the satisfaction of mastering such an intricate skill is its own reward, not to mention the apples, pears, and attractive trees that result from good husbandry. Though the espalier is a reminder to reconsider those Old World gardening techniques that have been used for centuries, it's also a statement of faith in the future.

VEGETABLES

I've included this section on vegetables to help convince you that it's a good idea to grow some of your own food, especially given our concern today with pesticides, herbicides, and food additives. Part of the purpose is also to introduce you to the story behind some familiar and not-so-familiar vegetables, and to show you that the vegetables we grow can be as rich in association with fellow gardeners as are our favorite flowers. The first chapter, "Mid-Season Planting," will be especially helpful, I hope, in showing that we can continue to plant seeds and seedlings even into August.

I include the final chapter, "Children in the Garden," by way of saying that we all need to involve our children in the act of designing, planting, and caring for the natural world. If they grow up knowing how to plant a radish, the future of this planet will be all that much brighter.

26

MID-SEASON PLANTING

June offers a brief period of calm for the gardener—a short spell when the crops are up in force but the weeds are not—and the last thing a gardener wants is the prospect of more planting. But consider the benefits of mid-season planting. It comes at a time when most of the soil preparation is completed. Many of the crops suggested for mid-season planting are leafy or root vegetables that require less attention than the fruit-bearing crops already growing in the garden. And because they are compact and hardy, they demand less space and time, yet they will fill the blank spots left in the garden after the early vegetables are harvested. They also add to your freezer and root cellar later in the fall.

But even given the relative ease of mid-season planting, July is the hottest month, and seedlings planted at this time of year require special care. Try to maintain even moisture levels in the soil by timely watering and applications of mulch. This will keep plants growing at a steady and healthy pace.

Avoid watering directly from a hose, since cold tap water can chill seedlings and temporarily stunt their growth. Instead, place a covered plastic barrel in an inconspicuous spot near the garden, and fill it periodically with water from the hose. The sun will warm the water, which can then be taken to the garden in a watering can.

One other piece of advice: Test your soil to determine what nutrients you need to add before planting specific mid-season crops. Soil depleted by earlier plants will hinder good, vigorous growth.

Most of the vegetables mentioned below are recent recommendations of Shepherd Ogden. Ogden puts out a culinary vegetable and herb seed catalog, *The Cook's Garden*, from his home in Londonderry, Vermont.

BUSH BEANS

Bush varieties of snap beans can be planted every two weeks during the growing season until seven to eight weeks before the first fall frost is expected. Although the beans you planted in spring will continue to produce crops until frost if you kept the young beans picked, a mid-season planting of a second or even a third crop will yield more tender and more bounteous beans. Planting the seeds two inches deep in the soil will protect them from the hot sun.

BEETS

The hot, dry conditions of midsummer cause beets to become tough and stringy, so harvest your first planting in early or mid July and plant another crop, which will flourish in the cooler weather of late summer. Beets will mature 55 to 60 days after sowing and can withstand the early fall frosts. Ample and steady moisture is essential to producing succulent beets. They require a soil with a pH of 6.0 or more. If you are in doubt about the pH, sprinkle ground limestone or wood ashes in the row at planting time.

Recommended beets are 'Long Keeper' and 'Lutz Green Leaf'.

BROCCOLI

Members of the cabbage family do best in cool, moist growing conditions and will withstand early fall frosts. Broccoli seeds can be sown in late June or early July in a nursery row or in containers from which they can be transplanted. In mid August the seedlings are set out in the garden two feet apart, but not where other members of the cabbage family have grown within three years. Thalassa Cruso notes that these seedlings do not mind hot weather, but "they will not change gears, as it were, and move into the stage where they become edible until the nights have begun to cool off." Once the seedlings have been put into the main garden, lettuce transplants can be set between them. The broccoli will be mature after two months; the lettuce, after one.

Other gardeners, such as the late James Underwood Crockett, opt for sowing the broccoli seeds directly into carefully prepared soil in early July. Plants in the cabbage family are finicky about soil pH—they do best at 6.6 to 7.5—so before sowing, add ground limestone to the soil. Crockett also added 10-10-10 fertilizer and about two inches of compost and dug them into the soil to the depth of the spading fork.

Recommended broccoli varieties are 'Romanesco', for mild winter areas, and 'Premium Crop', an F_1 hybrid.

CABBAGE

In the North, if you have not started your own seedlings in May, check with your local nursery for seedlings of fall-maturing varieties such as 'Danish Ball Head' or savoy varieties such as 'Savoy Ace' (F_1) or 'Blue Max'. These plants will take anywhere from 85 to 100 days to reach maturity. If you live in Zones 9 or 10 where the temperature rarely falls below 30 degrees Fahrenheit, sow the seeds directly outdoors in mid August for a midwinter harvest.

CHINESE CABBAGE

In the North, 'Bok Choy' and 'Wong Bok' must be planted in mid season. If they are planted too early and the seedlings are exposed to cold temperature, they will produce flower stalks rather than heads in the heat of summer. The seeds can be sown from mid July to mid August or at least three months before the first fall frost is due. If you live in the South, you can sow a crop in the fall for an early spring harvest.

Prepare your soil with care. These vegetables need rich, moist soil that is high in organic matter and is nearly neutral. I dig in at least two inches of compost and add a dusting of ground limestone before sowing seeds. Later you should thin the seedlings to 18-inch intervals. Johnny's Selected Seeds in Albion, Maine, suggests 'China King' (F_1), 'Superior Danish', 'Two Seasons' (F_1), or 'Dynasty' (F_1) for mid-season planting.

CARROTS

The key to choosing the right carrot variety is to understand the nature of your soil. If your garden is sandy loam and you are prepared to loosen the soil down a foot or so, choose the long, slender varieties like 'A-Plus' or 'Touchon Deluxe'. If you have heavy, shallow soil, choose the stockier varieties such as 'Planet' or any of the 'Chantenay' types. All of these will mature in about 70 days. When sowing the seeds, mix in some radish seeds, which sprout quickly and will mark your rows. When carrot greens are six to eight inches high, scatter 5-10-10 along both sides of the rows. After fertilizing, pull the soil around the shoulders of each carrot to prevent green tops. If you live in Zones 9 or 10, you can sow carrot seeds in late summer.

CAULIFLOWER

This vegetable is not one of the easier ones to grow. It's best planted in mid season because maturing in hot summer months causes it to go by quickly. Cauliflower requires cool temperatures, constant moisture, and frequent fertilizer. Start the seeds in mid June so that the seedlings are ready to set out in late July. Four- to five-week-old seedlings will reach maturity in just over 50 days. When the developing head reaches the size of an apple, loosely tie the outer leaves over the head to cover it, thus blanching the curds. 'Snow Crown' (F_1) is a good variety for planting in mid season. It matures earlier than the 'Snowball' types and appears to be highly reliable. If you live in Zones 9 or 10, plant cauliflower as a winter or spring crop. Remember, cauliflower is a member of the cabbage family, so don't set it out where it or other family members have grown within three years.

CHARD

Swiss chard is a remarkably hardy leafy plant that can be sown in the spring garden and can be harvested through most of the summer and early fall. Swiss chard resists the ravages of heat, drought, and even frost. If you didn't plant any in the spring, or if you did and you want to rejuvenate the supply, plant some more in late July. 'Fordhook Giant' is a good variety to consider for stems, while 'Perpetual Spinach' is best for leaves. If you continue to harvest the outer leaves regularly, you'll have greens well into October, even in the North. If you live in the South, sow seeds in the fall for harvesting in two months.

COLLARDS AND KALE

These hardy greens are grown in the South, primarily as a substitute for the cool-weather-loving cabbage. In the more southern climates, seeds are sown in late summer and the leaves harvested two to three months later. Northern gardeners should plant a crop in early July. Both collards, with their smooth leaves, and kale, with ruffled leaves, withstand heavy frosts. They will be ready for harvesting after the early frosts have killed off most of the other leafy vegetables.

If you don't have room in your garden at mid season, you might want to sow seeds of collards or kale in a seedbed or in flats a month before setting them out in the garden. Prepare the soil as you would for broccoli, and set the two-inch-tall seedlings at three-inch intervals. In August, thin them to leave six inches between plants, adding the thinnings to your tossed salads. Plants will need another thinning in late August, to their final 18- to 24-inch spacing. Spreading 10-10-10 when thinning encourages rapid growth.

Recommended varieties are 'Vates'-type collard and kale.

CORN

The days to maturity of sweet corn range from 64 in 'Blitz' to 94 in 'Silver Queen', making it possible to sow on one date in spring and have an extended period of harvest. However, successive plantings of a favorite variety can be made every two weeks until the appropriate number of days before frost. To insure good pollination, remember to plant corn in blocks rather than in a single, long row.

CUCUMBERS

If your first crop of cucumbers tends to cease production in late August, sow another hill in early July to be sure you'll get young, tender cukes right up until the first frost. Allow about two months from seeding for cucumbers to bear fruit. To save space, grow the vines up a fence or trellis, or grow bush varieties such as 'Spacemaster'. These take up much less space than vining varieties. Abundant moisture and a scattering of 5-10-5 around each hill every two or three weeks will help.

ENDIVE AND ESCAROLE

The seeds of these slightly pungent salad greens can be sown at mid season. They take about 90 days to reach maturity, but the finely cut and curled leaves of endive or the broader, slightly twisted lettuce-like leaves of escarole can both withstand frost. If the leaves mature in midsummer, they taste more bitter than those that mature in cooler weather. Blanching with wide boards along either side of the row will also reduce the bitterness of escarole. If you don't have room in the garden, start the seeds for endive and escarole in plastic trays. Then, when the seedlings are two or three inches high and you have room, transplant them into the main garden.

Recommended varieties are 'Fine Curled' endive, and 'Batavian'-type, or 'Cornet'-type escarole.

KOHLRABI

This is another member of the cabbage family that grows best if planted in mid season and allowed to mature in cooler weather. In the North, the seeds can be sown up until the end of July. The plants like a rich and fertile soil and will mature in just under eight weeks. To assure healthy and tender tubers, keep the soil evenly moist, mulching if there is scant rainfall. Harvest when the tuber is around 2½ inches in diameter.

If you live in the South, sow seeds at two-week intervals beginning in mid August. If you don't have room in the garden at this time but expect to in two or three weeks, sow seeds in pots for later transplanting.

Recommended are white or purple 'Vienna'.

LETTUCE

For mid-season plantings of lettuce, choose any of the slow-bolting varieties: 'Orfeo' or 'Buttercrunch' are two examples. If you transplant lettuce in July or early August, give the plants more shade than you might have given your spring transplants. This will reduce the wilting caused by loss of water. Because many of the looseleaf lettuces mature in 45 to 50 days, you can plant seeds or seedlings up until early September in northern climates. 'Winter Marvel' and 'Arctic King' are recommended.

ONIONS

Although they need a relatively long time to mature, onions do have a place in the mid-season planting schedule. Seeds of hardy white bunching onions or scallions can be sown around July 1. 'Evergreen Long Whites', for example, will take about 60 days to reach edible size. If you don't harvest all of them, and you live in the more northerly regions of the country, winter them over under six inches of mulch for an early-spring crop.

PEAS

Those pea pods and the peas within them that mature in cool rather than hot weather are tastier and crisper, according to Jim Crockett. He always sowed a crop in early August of 'Lincoln' or 'Wando'. Peas are susceptible to high temperatures, and 'Wando' was developed to withstand relatively hot conditions. Both peas for shelling and the edible-podded varieties will grow to maturity in 65 to 75 days. Shepherd Ogden recommends 'Novella II', a bush pea. Remember to fertilize peas with a low-nitrogen fertilizer because peas are legumes and can obtain nitrogen from the atmosphere.

RADISHES

Summer radishes are such fast growers that seeds can be sown virtually anytime during the growing season up until a month before the first frosts. For best results, radishes should be grown quickly and with plenty of moisture. If the soil dries out and growth is checked, the vegetables will become hot, tough, and pithy. They also go into excess leaf production in very hot weather. Radishes benefit from an application of 10-10-10 fertilizer at planting time. Sprinkle some diazinon on the soil to prevent their being attacked by cabbage root maggots. 'Easter Egg' and 'China Rose' are good mid-season varieties; sow seeds in early and mid August.

Daikon radishes can also be sown in mid season. These are white, long-rooted, milder radishes that can be stored in the root cellar like carrots. 'Round Black Spanish' is another winter radish, up to four inches in diameter with black skin and white flesh. In the South, start successive plantings of both summer and winter radishes in the fall.

RUTABAGAS

Rutabagas are meant to be planted in midsummer. If they mature in the heat of June or July, they become bitter and tough. If you like this swede turnip, plant the seeds in early or mid July. They'll be ready for harvesting after one or two frosts, which improve their taste. Do not plant rutabagas near other members of the cabbage family, or where members of the cabbage family were planted the previous year.

SPINACH

Spinach is also a cool-weather plant; it tends to bolt in hot weather. Because many varieties of spinach reach maturity within 40 to 50 days, they can be planted in late August. 'Tyee' is especially good. 'Melody Hybrid' comes to maturity in 42 days, and 'Indian Summer' matures in 40 days. The latter is a good bolt-resistant variety and can be planted from late July into early August. For one of your later sowings, try 'Cold Resistant Savoy', a crinkle-leaved variety that should be planted sometime during late August and early September, depending on how far north you live. 'Cold Resistant Savoy' can also be wintered-over and harvested the following spring. In regions with much warmer climates, start plantings in the fall.

BRUSSELS SPROUTS

If you require a low-salt diet, you might want to plant this low-sodium vegetable long favored by English gardeners. Frost improves the flavor of the sprouts. If you can find them, sow seeds of 'Valiant' (F_1) or 'Silverstar' (F_1) immediately in pots. Otherwise plan to buy seedlings. Having prepared the soil as you would for broccoli, transplant the seedlings in mid July. Planting bolt-resistant lettuce seedlings between the young plants will give you a bit more space elsewhere for other mid-season planting.

TURNIPS

There is an old saying regarding this vegetable that underscores its role in the mid-season planting schedule in the Northeast: "On the twenty-fifth of July, sow your turnips wet or dry." Like rutabagas, turnips are a cool-season crop meant for late fall harvesting. If you enjoy not only the turnip but its greens as well, 'Shogoin' is a good variety. Within 30 to 40 days you'll have both turnips and greens. Another good variety is 'Des Vertus Marteau'.

27

GILFEATHER TURNIP

The turnip is generally regarded as a lowly vegetable. In seed catalogs it's relegated to a fifth of a column near the back and is invariably preceded by page after splashy page of photographs of plump, red tomatoes. Rarely is there a picture of a 'Purple Top' or 'Shogoin'. Even 'Tokyo Cross Hybrid' rarely gets its profile printed. Most people consider the turnip vulgar—put it in a stew and it becomes obtrusively so.

While the rest of us grow a row or two so that we can fill one serving dish at Thanksgiving dinner, a handful of gardeners in southeastern Vermont have been quietly raising turnips for 50 years. The variety they grow is called the Gilfeather turnip. Here's the story of this vegetable, a story that took me nearly four months to piece together.

One day, Al Lynch, a friend and fellow gardener, gave me a Gilfeather turnip. Not really liking turnip all that much, but pleased to have an indigenous Vermont vegetable, I took it home. After all, not many states can claim their own vegetable.

The unattractive, oblong root had a rough skin, quite unlike that of a good 'Tokyo Cross Hybrid'. I put it in the cellar and there it sat with the 'Hubbard' squash and potatoes for a week or more. Both my wife and I found it difficult to get excited about cooking the thing.

A week or so later I asked Al how best to cook it. He suggested boiling equal amounts of potato and turnip and then mashing them together. We did so, but before mixing them we tasted the turnip and discovered that the white root had a delicate flavor. The texture was smooth, and when mashed with spuds it further sweetened our already sweet 'Green Mountain' potatoes.

The next time I saw Al I told him how pleasantly surprised we were at the taste of his turnip. He wasn't surprised. He's heard that same response time and again. I asked him where he bought the seeds. "Bought? I don't think you can buy them. I got mine from my brother-in-law up in Dummerston."

I casually asked around for a few weeks, hoping to come across seeds for sale somewhere. I asked a few friends in Brattleboro, but I couldn't help feeling from the response I got that it was like asking them for directions to the pool in the West River where they caught that 16-inch trout. My curiosity was piqued.

I started asking around in earnest. People mentioned that they had gotten their seeds from a brother, an aunt in West Dover, an old guy in Guilford, a neighbor, or, "I can't remember. Seems as though there's been a jar of seeds in the cellar for years."

Finally the trail got warm. I asked Ernie Clark, a gardener and lifetime resident of Vermont. He said, "Give Flossy Howe at Agway a call." I did. She wasn't in, but the man I spoke to suggested I get in touch with Mary Lou Schmidt, out in Dummerston. I did, and that was when the hard news started coming in.

THE SCHMIDTS' FARM

One Saturday, at the Schmidts' invitation, I drove up to their 140-acre farm in the hills a few miles north of Brattleboro. From the kitchen where we sat I could look out of their impeccably maintained 200-year-old Cape through an alley of black locusts and across a sloping hayfield. Wooded hills and valleys formed overlapping horizons far in the distance. It was the kind of landscape that likely attracted Rudyard Kipling, who supposedly said that his two favorite cities in the world were Bombay and Brattleboro.

Mary Lou Schmidt told me that she used to raise registered Morgan horses on the property before turning her attention to managing the farm, with its Christmas tree plantation, maple grove, vegetable gardens, and timber and cordwood operations. One day in the spring of 1975, Cliff Emery, a neighbor, stopped by to see how the Schmidts' garden was doing. As so many of us do when we visit fellow gardeners in the spring,

Emery took along a container of seeds—he thought the Schmidts might not have any Gilfeather turnips. He was right.

Like most people, they weren't wild about turnip, but since Mary Lou and Bill appreciate a varied garden, they planted the tiny seeds, following Cliff's instructions, half an inch deep in mid July. They got what appeared to be 100-percent germination. Bill interrupted the story to say that the seeds grow virtually anywhere.

After the turnips had been sweetened by two or three October frosts, Bill brought a few in from the garden and they began to experiment with various ways of cooking them. They put chunks into stews and found that the Gilfeather added a subtle sweetness rather than the slightly bitter taste of most turnips. Mary Lou added, "I'll never make mashed potatoes without them again, and children like this turnip, too."

Mary Lou called Cliff Emery, hoping she could trace the development of the Gilfeather turnip. Cliff had lived in Dummerston for over 50 years; surely he would know where to buy seeds. But they were not for sale anywhere. One could only get them over the garden fence. According to Cliff, the turnips and seeds had been around southeastern Vermont for as long as he could remember.

Being enthusiastic farmers, the Schmidts wanted to promote the indigenous vegetable, and its rightful name, for their state. They began a process by which they hoped to have the vegetable registered as an official Vermont plant.

They started by investigating the history of the Gilfeather turnip. They got in touch with the then owner of Gilfeather farm, in Wardsboro, the late Dr. Courtney Bishop, a retired professor of clinical surgery at Yale and chief of staff at Yale-New Haven hospital. Bill asked Dr. Bishop what he knew about the Gilfeather family and the turnip named for them. Dr. Bishop recounted that the Gilfeather family came from County Fermanaugh, Ireland, to New York, by way of the sailing ship *Orient* out of Liverpool. They arrived in March 1863, and went to stay with relatives in Manchester, Vermont. In 1870, they purchased the farm high above the village of Wardsboro. John Gilfeather was the eldest of the seven children. He never married but lived with his brother William in the family homestead.

MR. GILFEATHER'S TURNIPS

Dr. Bishop said that no one who lives in Wardsboro knows how or when John developed the turnip. Some do remember, however, that he would drive a pair of horses down from his mountainside farm one day late each October. The draft horses would be pulling a wagon whose bed was loaded to the brim with turnips. John would spend a long day driving the 60-mile round trip to Brattleboro and back to sell his crop. Because the turnip is biennial, those who bought the Gilfeather variety would store them in the cellar and replant them in the spring. By late July or early August the three-foot flower stalks would have produced hundreds of ripened seed pods.

John Gilfeather was a respected citizen and a successful farmer. He was a town selectman as well as a representative from his district to the state legislature in Montpelier. At the age of 73, he sold his farm to a professor of physics at Columbia University and moved down to the village of Wardsboro. He died of pneumonia in 1944 at the age of 79.

THE GILFEATHER GOES TO MARKET

In the fall of 1979 the Schmidts were well into their trial plantings and had experienced complete success with germination. In fact, they had given Felix Blum, a friend from Guilford, a packet of seeds. A few weeks after planting them, Felix ran into Mary Lou. She asked how his turnip seeds had done. "Ninety-five-percent germination—that's what you said, right? Well, it's more like 150 percent. I've got turnips all over the place." Knowing, too, that the turnip wintered over successfully under no more than a few inches of mulch, the Schmidts were more than ever convinced of the potential of this unique and delicately flavored turnip.

They wrote to the Vermont Department of Agriculture in Montpelier, requesting information on how to market the seeds and were directed to the University of Vermont, where their seeds were tested for purity of strain and percentage of germination. By early 1980 the Schmidts had fulfilled all the requirements of the Vermont Department of Weights and Measures and were allowed to market the seeds, but only within the state. They could be sold under the name of Vermont Gilfeather Turnip. Mary Lou took the first 150 packets of seeds to Flossy Howe, at Agway. They were put on display in midwinter and sold out in 10 days. Before the end of April, the entire stock of seeds for the 1980 growing season was sold out.

Bill wrote a two-paragraph announcement for *Agriview*, a bulletin for Vermont farmers. The piece, entitled "Gilfeather Turnip Seeds Available," brought immediate and enthusiastic responses from all over Vermont, New Hampshire, and upper New York state.

Greatly encouraged by this reaction, the Schmidts began looking into registering the plant with the U.S. Department of Agriculture (USDA). They wrote to Washington and three days later received an enthusiastic phone call from an official of the Plant Variety and Protection Division. He was only too happy to help them apply for the registration of this "heirloom variety." Bill marveled at the efficient response from the giant bureaucracy. "Washington was so helpful. I'm encouraged to know that at least part of the federal bureaucracy can be personal, direct, and helpful."

A few days after the phone call, a packet of forms arrived in the mail. After submitting the completed forms, the Schmidts were required to send in a drawing of the plant and its root system, a field description, and a formal botanical description (with which the people at the University of Vermont helped). Just after the plants formed mature seed pods, an entire specimen had to be pulled up and sent to Washington, along with a packet of seeds. They also sent Dr. Bishop's historical material on the Gilfeather family.

In October 1980, the Schmidts received a letter from the USDA: Mr. Gilfeather's turnip was indeed a unique vegetable. The plant specimen and seeds had been registered and sent to the vaults of the National Seed Storage Laboratory, in Fort Collins, Colorado. This means that the Schmidts can now sell the seed nationwide. (They have since trademarked the name "Gilfeather.") If you would like a 1.8-gram packet, send $1 and a self-addressed, stamped envelope to Elysian Hills, R.R. 5, Box 452, Brattleboro, Vermont 05301. The Schmidts are more than certain that this hardy and adaptable turnip can grow anywhere other turnips succeed.

Gilfeather turnip, an heirloom vegetable from Vermont, is hardy and adaptable anywhere other turnips grow. It's uglier than most, but far sweeter.

After four months of searching for the story of this modest turnip, both my wife and I felt a kind of attachment to it and the people growing it. We had left only one leaf unturned—a visit to the Bishops and Gilfeather Farm.

One day, during a February thaw, we arranged to visit the Bishops. We drove to the village, only to be met in the valley by Dr. Bishop in his four-wheel-drive vehicle.

"Pretty steep and muddy," we were warned. "Better come with me." We parked our car down by Whetstone Brook bridge and climbed into the sturdy Jeep. As the doctor drove up the hill, the views got more and more breath taking. After a few moments we arrived at the farm perched on the hillside. We walked through the barn that had once been the stable for John's draft horses, and then stopped by a spring that trickled from under a rock outcropping by the back door of the house. From where we stood, we could look down to the lower hayfields and Mrs. Bishop's reasonably level garden, then out to the Windham hills stretching into the distance. Or we could turn around and look up at the steeply sloping upper hayfields. "Not a square inch of level ground on the place, it seems," Dr. Bishop said. He knew; he'd been cutting and baling hay on a tractor with half-tracks for 30 years.

Mrs. Bishop welcomed us into her home and, having placated our then two-year-old son with a miniature wood stove and utensils, she launched into the story of her experiences with the turnip. In 1950, when she and Dr. Bishop bought the Gilfeather farm, she asked around for seeds of the turnip. She heard that a gardener in Newfane, some 10 miles or so from Wardsboro, sold the turnips. She looked him up and asked if he would sell her some seeds. "No" was the reply. He would sell her some turnips, however. When she got home she discovered the tops and bottoms were so severely cut back that they could not possibly give rise to roots or flower stalks. A year or so later she discovered Leona Cobb, who had worked for Mr. Gilfeather. Leona Cobb supplied her with some seeds, and the Bishops went on to raise five 90-foot rows of turnips in the very soil in which John Gilfeather grew them.

Every fall for years people drove up the dead-end dirt road to buy turnips by the bushel. "And you know," she continued, "even with all those rows I never have enough. They're awful looking things, but people sure do like them. By the way, don't ever cook them in aluminum. They turn gray."

We chatted about John Gilfeather, the farm, and its history, and then Mrs. Bishop added one last little teaser to a mystery I thought had been solved. A few years earlier she and Dr. Bishop were visiting their daughter and her family, near Wiesbaden, West Germany. One day they were walking through a local market when she was pulled up short by the sight of what looked very much like Gilfeather turnips. She remembered that old-timers in Wardsboro had told her that John frequently referred to his turnip as a white, sweet German turnip. They bought one and cooked it for dinner. It tasted very much like the Gilfeather.

Clearly, the next step for us is to fly to Wiesbaden to talk with the market gardeners in the area. But, then, perhaps some reader can shed further light on this subject and save us the trip.

28 🌼

SALSIFY

My wife and I plant certain vegetables for the associations they hold. Scarlet runner beans and broad beans are in our garden this season so that we can enjoy some sturdy beans that conjure up memories of her parents' farm in England. When we sit down to a meal that includes salsify (*Tragopogon porrifolius*), we think of our friends Jean and Hellen Gazagnaire, who introduced us to this delicately flavored root vegetable a few years ago. They were both born in France, where salsify is a popular vegetable.

Jean, who was raised in Paris in the 1930s, remembers walking to the market in Montmartre with his mother. Then, as now, rue Lepic was a market street a fifth of a mile long, connecting place Blanche with la Butte. On Saturday or Sunday, Jean and his mother would walk the length of rue Lepic, shopping. Some vendors displayed food and housewares in front of their homes or inside their shops, while others sold from two-wheeled carts set up on the curbs. If it was October or November, Jean and his mother might stop at a greengrocer's to buy salsify. (The slender eight-inch roots were rarely in the markets before then.) The grocer would remove all but an inch or so of the greens from the creamy-white, somewhat hairy roots. Then he would tie them in small bunches and wrap them in a sheet of newspaper. A grocer might use *Le Journal*, *Petit Parisien*, *Le Figaro*, or *L'Intransigent*, depending on his politics.

Jean said that the roots probably came from the market gardens of central or northern France, where the soil is generally lighter than the stony soil of the south. Salsify requires a light, friable soil that allows it to grow unhindered down through the earth.

THE OYSTER PLANT

Salsify is sometimes called oyster plant, because the taste of the cooked root reminds many people of that mollusk. It is this delicate flavor that makes the vegetable so popular in western Europe. Salsify is native to the eastern Mediterranean region; the ancient Greeks and Romans gathered it from the wild. It was cultivated in French and German gardens as early as the 1500s, and considered a common field herb in England by the eighteenth century. *Tragopogon porrifolius* escaped cultivation after it was introduced in this country and can be found growing wild from southern Canada south to Georgia, Tennessee, and Missouri. Early American settlers prized salsify, but gradually it fell out of favor.

Gardeners certainly cannot fault seed companies for salsify's lack of popularity. Look into almost any catalog and you will find 'Mammoth Sandwich Island' salsify seed for sale. The plant is relatively easy to grow. I grew it in our sandy, nearly neutral soil. If your soil, like ours, produces good parsnips or the longer types of carrots, you can certainly grow this hardy biennial. It's relatively disease- and pest-resistant.

SOWING THE SEEDS

Sow the seeds as soon as the soil can be worked in the spring, well before the last frost. I have found that salsify needs about 120 days to mature, but some experts say 150. Gardeners in Zone 3 should plant seed as early in the spring as possible. If you live in a zone with appreciably fewer than 120 frost-free days, try planting the seeds in mid September, wintering-over the seedlings under six to eight inches of mulch. If the root grows much larger than pencil-size in the fall, however, it will bolt the following spring and will be of no use for eating. And its foliage is so hardy that even after three or four frosts in autumn, you'll see the crisp, leek-like leaves (*porrifolius* means "with leaves like a leek's") standing healthy and green. While the rest of the garden is a brown and untidy place, the salsify stands as a heartening reminder of what has been.

People in the warmer climates of the U.S. and Canada have

more difficulty than those in the northern zones getting salsify seed to germinate and grow. In general, salsify prefers temperatures between 55 and 75 degrees Fahrenheit. If you have failed to get good germination, try soaking the seeds for 48 hours, then setting them between wet paper towels. Keep the towels moist and at room temperature during the day, and put them in the refrigerator at night. After four or five days, radicles, or rudimentary roots, should appear. When they are about half an inch long, plant them gently in your garden.

Before you sow the seeds, sprouted or not, prepare the soil to a depth of a foot or more. Loosen the soil with a spade and remove any rocks you find. Because salsify does best in a neutral or nearly neutral soil, you might add limestone or wood ashes if your soil is highly acidic. You should also add well-decomposed compost or manure. Be sure not to add fresh manure, as it may cause forked or otherwise misshapen roots. If you have a heavy soil that is peppered with rocks, or if it has so much clay or silt that it hardens or packs when dry, lighten it by mixing in generous amounts of sharp sand and compost.

Plant the seeds an inch deep, a couple of inches apart, in rows that are about 18 inches apart. When the seedlings are two or three inches high, they will look like wisps of grass. This characteristic has led to the undoing of many a salsify planting: an overzealous weeder uproots the seedlings, thinking they are blades of grass. To acquaint yourself with the appearance of the young seedlings, plant several seeds in a pot indoors a few days before sowing seed outdoors.

When the leaves are three or four inches high, thin the plants to four inches apart. Like most root vegetables, salsify grows best at an even pace. Dry periods can slow its growth and make the harvested root less tender. In periods of drought, water deeply. To keep the ground as evenly moist as possible, mulch the rows with leaves or lawn clippings.

HARVESTING AND STORING

When the roots are an inch or two wide at the shoulders, they are ready to be harvested. If you live in one of the colder zones of North America, leave the roots in the ground until they have been exposed to two or three frosts—the roots will be sweeter for it. Loosen the soil along the row with a spading fork or shovel, and pull the plants out as you would carrots.

Depending on the severity of the winter in your area, choose from among three methods of storing salsify. The roots retain their flavor best if left in the ground, so mulch the rows with six to eight inches of hay or straw if your winters won't freeze the ground solid under the mulch. Then you can simply dig up what you want throughout the winter. Or you can dig up the roots, remove all but an inch or so of the leaves, and store the roots in moist sand in the cellar, just as you would carrots. The third choice is to freeze the roots. Scrape the skins, cut the roots into four-inch sections, and drop them into water acidulated with lemon juice. Once you have prepared enough for freezing, blanch the roots for a minute, cool, place in containers, and freeze.

If you leave some of the mature salsify roots in the soil until the next spring, dig them for eating before new leaf growth is six inches high. After that the roots become virtually inedible. You will find, however, that the shoot arising from the crown can be harvested when it's about four inches high. These shoots, cooked like asparagus, make a fine vegetable.

If you allow the year-old shoots to grow, by early summer a sturdy, well-branched, two- to three-foot stalk will develop and produce an abundance of light-purple flowers that close at noon. This habit explains why in England salsify is sometimes called John-go-to-bed-at-noon. As Gerard's *Herball*, published in 1597, notes, "when these floures be come to their full maturitie and ripenesse they grow into a downy Blow-ball like those of dandelion, which is carried away with the winde." Salsify is also called goatsbeard, owing to the long silky beard, or pappus, attached to the mature seeds. This trait is common to many other plants in the Compositae family as well.

BLACK SALSIFY

Black salsify, or scorzonera (*Scorzonera hispanica*), is another root vegetable that looks and tastes a good deal like salsify, and it is a member of the same family. *Scorzonera* is a genus of more than 100 species of Old World herbaceous plants, but the only species of any interest to gardeners is *S. hispanica*. Its common

Closely associated with Europe, salsify has a taste reminiscent of oysters and will add a new dimension to your vegetable garden and your table.

name, naturally, refers to the black skin of the root. It gets it Latin name from the Italian word *scorzonera*, meaning "viper's plant," because it was once thought to provide an antidote for snakebites. In Old French *scorzone* means serpent. In Germany the plant is called *schwarzwurzel*, meaning "black root." During the Middle Ages, this vegetable was thought to be a remedy against smallpox. Louis XIV is said to have had his gardeners plant scorzonera because he felt it helped relieve his indigestion. The vegetable was widely grown throughout Europe until Victorian times, when fastidious cooks found that peeling the black root was dirty work. Hellen Gazagnaire can remember peeling black salsify roots with her mother. "Our hands did get quite sticky and black. We found it most disagreeable." Nevertheless, it's worth growing. Cooks often cite its more pronounced oyster flavor, one that many prefer over that of the salsify root.

Scorzonera can be distinguished easily from salsify by its broader leaves, its yellow flowers, and its perennial (rather than biennial) nature. Like salsify, scorzonera is grown primarily as an annual. It is cultivated and cooked in almost all respects like salsify. Only one difference exists: scorzonera can be left in the ground for a second season to increase its yield. We tried this over the past two years and found that the second-season root was larger than the first season's, but just as tender.

Seeds of black salsify are widely available. We used Johnny's Selected Seeds 'Gigantia' and have found it to be very good. The Thompson and Morgan catalog notes that scorzonera makes a good companion plant for carrots, since it is thought to repel carrot fly. You might try mixing the seeds of the two plants and then sowing in the same row, thinning to four inches later on.

Not many Americans have tasted salsify or scorzonera, so you may find growing it and serving it a particular pleasure. Salsify, for all its unassuming nature, can enrich our experience at the table as well as in the garden.

29

ASPARAGUS

My father had been growing apples, peaches, and pears for 15 years with great patience when, in 1943, he decided to put in a quarter acre of asparagus. He began a process that would take at least three years to come to fruition. Having dug the trenches, he lined them with well-decomposed cow manure and planted the one-year-old 'Mary Washington' roots. Other than hoeing and fertilizing, he left the bed to its own devices for two years. Then, following the traditional harvesting schedule, he cut for two weeks during the third year, four weeks during the fourth year, and six weeks during the fifth and subsequent years. During those six weeks, people would drive up the winding dirt road to our hilltop farm to buy the 30 to 40 pounds my parents cut each morning before the summer sun shone on the spears.

In 1950, the town of New Hartford, Connecticut, decided to tar the road, and herein lies my first distinct memory of asparagus. In the process of laying the road, they covered about a third of the asparagus bed with six to eight inches of gravel and then covered that with a layer of tar and sand. But the asparagus was not deterred. As we cut during subsequent springs, I marveled at how the delicate tips rose unharmed through the tar and gravel. Sometimes spears supported whole chunks of it. We eventually stopped tending the bed for the same reason that most people do: the rooty system became bound in grass, morning-glory, and weed roots, and, as a result, the patch virtually stopped producing. My father told me, however, that even 25 years after he abandoned the bed, asparagus was still coming up at the edge of the road.

FUSARIUM ROT

The root system of asparagus is extensive. The fleshy storage roots, pencil thick and anywhere from 5 to 10 feet in length, grow out of a rhizome commonly known as the crown. Feeder rootlets that grow along the length of the storage roots gather water and nutrients from the soil, while the fern-like stalks produce carbohydrates and other nutrients. The storage roots hold this supply of food until it's required in the spring for the production of spears, stalks, and thus seeds.

If the work done by the foliage is impaired by pests, or if the delicate feeder rootlets are attacked by disease or fungi, or must compete with weeds and grasses, then the storage roots cannot provide enough spears for harvesting. During the 1970s, asparagus beds across America—particularly in California, New Jersey, and Massachusetts—were attacked by fusarium crown rot, a fungal infection that severely reduced production. For example, before 1973, the year that significant fusarium fungus appeared in Hadley, Massachusetts, Wallace Hibbard and his son Ernest were harvesting 125 24-pound boxes of asparagus an acre. By the early 1980s they were down to 30 boxes an acre.

In the early 1970s at Rutgers University in New Jersey, Dr. J. Howard Ellison and his colleague Dr. Stephen Garrison began a hybridizing program in hopes of developing a strain that was resistant to fusarium wilt. They introduced the 'Beacon' and 'California' strains in the mid 1970s but those proved only partially resistant. In 1980 Ernest Hibbard told me, "If a resistant strain isn't found soon, we'll be out of business." Much to the relief of the Hibbards and growers like them all across America, Dr. Ellison and his colleagues did develop a more resistant hybrid, called 'Jersey Giant'. It's been commercially available for the last four years and every indication is that it will be a great boon to commerical growers and home gardeners.

Several attributes of 'Jersey Giant' help make it "a giant step forward for the asparagus industry," in the words of John Howell, who works for the Extension Service at the University of Massachusetts. First, it's highly resistant to the fusarium fungus. Second, it's a male hybrid, which means that none of the plant's energy goes into seed production but rather into the development of larger ferns and thereby larger spears the following spring.

Howell notes that "walking through a field of 'Jersey Giant' ferns five or six feet tall in August is like the good old days." Acreage and per-acre production are up dramatically. Howell says, "Ten years ago we had between 100 and 150 acres in asparagus production in our area. We've more than doubled that figure, and it has to do with confidence in 'Jersey Giant'. After all, a good grower can get upwards of 250 or 300 boxes per acre now. If any home gardeners have been waiting to plant asparagus, now is the time." (Tim Nourse of South Deerfield, Massachusetts, is an excellent source.)

BUYING AND PLANTING

Young crowns are by far the best to plant, according to Paul Harlow, an organic grower in southern Vermont. He recommends that you buy one-year-old roots—between 10 and 15 for each adult in your family. The younger roots have an abundance of fine, fibrous feeder rootlets. Two- and even three-year-old roots are available from garden centers or catalogs, but when old roots are dug from nursery beds, Harlow points out, much of the root structure is severed or damaged. This already slow-growing plant takes a long time to recover from the shock of transplanting, whereas a younger plant recovers much more quickly and, in the long term, will produce more spears more quickly.

The bed in which the roots are to be planted should be prepared with care. Ideally, one shoud select a light, loamy soil with good drainage. After digging a trench that is 10 inches deep and 18 inches wide, line it with four inches of well-decomposed compost or cow manure, plus 10-10-10 fertilizer at the rate of one-half pound to each 10-foot stretch of trench. Add ground limestone as needed to get the pH level up to around 7.0. Add some topsoil, dig it all in together, and then tamp down the mixture. You should have a six-inch-deep trench left.

Now it's time to plant the roots, and here lies something of a controversy—how deep should they be set? Harlow mentioned during our conversation that in 1950 his father planted roots at a depth of about 18 inches. Both Paul and his father feel that of all the beds on their farm, it yielded the thickest and most abundant spears; furthermore, it produced well for 25 years. Yet other growers believe that beds planted at depths of anywhere from two to eight inches are equally successful.

John Howell told me that the U.S. Department of Agriculture recently began discouraging people from the practice of deep planting. A USDA bulletin has this to say:

"Deep planting of crowns, formerly a general practice, is no longer recommended. In loose, light, organic soil, crowns should be planted deeper than in heavier mineral soils. Most commercial plantings in light soils are made at a depth of about eight inches. In mineral soils it is doubtful whether it is good practice to set deeper than four inches. Experiments in Massachusetts in mineral soil showed that the loss of plants after setting increased from 11 percent at four inches to 34 percent at eight inches."

In general, Howell suggests planting roots at a depth of between four and six inches. He adds that research suggests the roots of *A. officinalis*, over a period of years, find their own proper depth for the soil in which they are growing.

Once you have resolved the question of planting depth to your own satisfaction, lay out the roots 18 inches on center. The buds of the crowns should point upward, the roots spreading out like a star. Cover the one-year-old root system with two inches of soil and then, over the course of the summer, periodically add more soil, so that by summer's end, the soil line in what was the trench is level with that of the garden's surface. Let the spears grow up into ferny fronds.

Resist all temptation to cut the spears. The fronds that they eventually give rise to are essential in building up an abundant food supply in the storage roots for later years.

ASPARAGUS AND SALT

Applying common salt to asparagus beds has long been a traditional practice. However, there is little scientific evidence to support this practice. Asparagus does have an unusually high tolerance for salt—it's known to grow along the edges of salt marshes—but the plant doesn't take in salt as a nutrient. "Good weed killer, salt," says Ernest Hibbard, "but that's about it." He doesn't advise putting salt on an asparagus bed, primarily because it could leach into adjoining beds or poison the soil in the bed itself. The plot would then be useless for other gardening in the event that the asparagus bed is taken up in later years. His advice? Keep salt out of the garden.

MAINTENANCE AND PEST CONTROL

There are a few other things to keep in mind. Don't let the young roots dry out. In dry periods, water them sufficiently to wet the soil to a depth of at least eight inches once a week. In later years, fertilize in April and again in late June just after the end of the harvest. Every fall, after you have cut the yellowed stalks and burned them, liberally spread decomposed cow manure on the bed.

Burning the stalks will help control the common and 12-spotted asparagus beetles, which lay their eggs on the browning stalks in the fall. In the spring, the new beetles, which hibernate for the winter under rubbish or leaves near the garden, emerge, feed on the tender shoots, and lay more eggs, thus beginning a new cycle. These eggs hatch into grubs, which attack the stalks, fronds, and even berries. Burning the stalks helps control the pest, but you may need to do more.

If you are averse to insecticides, you might consider buying some poultry as an alternative control method. Let them run free in the asparagus patch, and they will do an excellent job of keeping the beetle population down. A second method of control is suggested by the Harlows. They allow spears at certain corners of their beds to grow to maturity at the very beginning of the season. The beetles are attracted to those plants, leaving the rest of the bed relatively free from the insect.

Now I hear you asking, after all that preparation and all that work, I can only harvest asparagus for two weeks that third year? Well, during those years between planting and harvesting, take solace in French author Marcel Proust's philosophy that much of our pleasure lies in anticipation.

HARVESTING AND COOKING

When the more tangible rewards of your patience do come to fruition in the early spring of that third year, they will be thick and tender specimens, much more so than they would have been if you had rushed the process. And take care with the harvesting. Don't compromise three years of patience with a knife. Snap the spears off as close to ground level as you can with your fingers. If you use a knife, you stand a good chance of harming the crown, the very source of life you have been so patiently allowing to mature.

If you've planted a generous number of roots, rest assured that you can freeze what you can't eat, thus spreading out that meager two weeks' cutting.

If the summer where you live is relatively hot and dry, you might enjoy drying the spears. In Pliny's time, the finest spears were dried. When the vegetable was needed for table, the dried spears were placed in boiling water and cooked for only a few moments. In fact, one of Emperor Augustus's favorite sayings was *Citus quam asparagi coquentur*, "Do it quicker than you can cook asparagus."

Though the Greeks never cultivated the plant, Dioscorides mentions that wild asparagus is of significant medicinal value, particularly as a diuretic. And Avicenna, the eleventh-century Arabian physician, said that eating the vegetable would make people "feel good throughout all of their bodies," though he does note that their urine would have a bad odor.

Pliny also mentions the nutritional value of asparagus, particularly insofar as it helps maintain the health of the eyes. Modern science bears him out on this point; a cup of cut asparagus contains 1,300 international units of vitamin A. Blanched asparagus, achieved by ridging the soil above the crowns, is almost devoid of vitamins.

As all lovers of asparagus know, the very best time to harvest is no more than an hour before cooking. I can remember as a boy going out to the patch in back of the barn with my father just before dinner. As we walked toward the asparagus bed, my mother would be putting the water on to boil. Ten minutes later we would be back with the spears and the water would be boiling. A few minutes later my two brothers, my parents, and I would sit down to a dinner of nothing but a loaf of homemade bread, butter, and a pound of asparagus each.

30 🌿

RHUBARB

In 1770, Benjamin Franklin was living in London as an agent for Massachusetts and a spokesman for the colonies. As was his wont, he held a multitude of interests. Even in those complex times five years before the American Revolution, he took the opportunity on January 11, 1770, to ship a crate of rhubarb roots, then relatively unknown in America, to John Bartram in Philadelphia.

Bartram (1699-1777) was a man to appreciate this crate of roots, for he was the preeminent botanist of his time and had served as honorary botanist under King George II. Bartram might well have planted those roots in Kingsessing, the botanical gardens he founded in 1725, which today are part of the Philadelphia park system. We might, then, tag 1770 as the year rhubarb was officially introduced into this country.

For almost 60 years, not many Americans used the plant for culinary purposes. One reason might be that people associated the plant with tincture of rhubarb, a strong laxative that grandmother might have forced on them.

We know from a late-nineteenth-century issue of *The American Naturalist* that our garden variety of rhubarb, *Rheum rhabarbarum*, appeared in the seed catalogs for the first time in 1828. By then it had won some degree of acceptance as a plant to be used in cooking.

By 1828, the rootstocks of various species of the genus *Rheum* had been used for medicinal purposes for over 4,000 years. The Chinese herbal *Pen-King*, believed to date from around 2700 B.C., mentions such use in China and Tibet. For centuries thereafter, the powder made from the dried rootstocks of *R. palmatum, R. officinale,* and other species was the base of a tincture that was valuable in the treatment of bacillary dysentery.

Lord Berners wrote in 1533 that "the physicions with a lyttell Rubarb purge many humours of the body." Shakespeare knew well the purgative powers of the plant. Just before Macbeth leaves the protection of Dunsinane for his final battle with Macduff and his English soldiers, he asks his doctor, "What rhubarb, senna, or what purgative drug would scour these English hence?"

Scientists tell us that the constituents giving rhubarb this purgative property and the yellow color of the rhizomes are anthracene glycosides. Nearly 40 percent of this drug consists of calcium oxalate. Rheotannic acid, an astringent, is also present; this is the constituent that dries your mouth after eating rhubarb.

It was not until the late 1600s that the stalks of *R. rhabarbarum* were used in the kitchens of European homes with any degree of interest. Even by 1820, rhubarb was not heartily accepted as an edible fruit in England. One of the first recorded commercial growers in that country was Joseph Myatt of Deptford. He took five bunches of stalks to the Borough Market that year and at the end of the day had to go home with two.

The present garden variety, *R. rhabarbarum*, is believed to have originated in the desert region of Siberia around the Volga River basin. Tournefort called the plant *rhabarbarum*. The name combines *Rha*, the name the Muscovites gave the Volga, with his notion that barbarous people lived in the region where the vegetable grew. *Rhabarbarum* was gradually shortened to *rhubarb*.

Being disease- and pest-resistant to a remarkable degree, this plant, a pie plant for New Englanders, is one of the least finicky, most hardy, longest living of garden perennials. Technically a vegetable, though used as a substitute for fruit in early spring, it is grown for its pleasantly acidic petioles, whose juice has a pH of 3.2. This makes it one of the more acidic plants in the garden.

RHUBARB'S PROPERTIES AS A SPRAY

The woody rhizomes and large storage roots with a mass of feeder roots comprise a complex root system. The storage roots, shaped somewhat like stout carrots, store nutrients that give rise to the beautifully pinkish red stalks in the early spring.

While the roots have been used medicinally and the stalks as a fruit, the leaves are not used because of their poisonous concentration of oxalic acid. Ingestion can cause gastroenteritis, and damage to the kidneys can result from the formation of calcium oxalate.

Though we know that the broad leaves were used to cover baskets of vegetables and fruits in European markets during the late nineteenth century, it is probably best to discard the leaves. They can safely go onto the compost heap.

The leaves do have two uses, however, according to the Henry Doubleday Research Association in Essex, England. They can be used to make a mild insecticide and a fungicide. The Association's booklet, *Pest Control without Poisons*, gives the following recipe for a mild insecticide: "Cut up three pounds of rhubarb leaves and boil in three quarts of water for thirty minutes. Strain and then add four ounces of liquid detergent or soap flakes, both of which serve equally well as a wetting agent." The liquid can then be used as a spray to control aphids.

Another recipe used for decades by Irish gardeners has proved effective against the fungus that causes clubroot in brassicas. Boil 1½ pounds of rhubarb leaves in a gallon of water for a half hour. Strain and pour the liquid into the holes in which you are about to plant cabbage or other brassicas. As an added measure, water with this liquid weekly. Some British gardeners even set three or four 1½-inch pieces of rhubarb around the bottom of the hole before planting. You might enjoy experimenting with these remedies yourself.

PLANTING AND HARVESTING

If you are thinking of putting in a few rhubarb plants, here are some thoughts on the subject culled from the experts. First, remember that while rhubarb is not finicky, it does require a period of dormancy. For this reason, the plant grows most successfully in northern climates. Stalks from plants in southerly regions are thin and green. Cool seasons and freezing winters are necessary to produce stalks with the delicate pink shade prized so highly by cooks.

As with all perennials, there are two ways to get rootstock: from your neighbors and friends in exchange for your prizes or from your nursery grower. The former is by far the more fun. If you have a friend who plans to separate a rhubarb plant in the spring, show up on the day with a sharp spade. Dig carefully to expose the root system. Using the sharp spade, cut straight down through the roots so that each section you separate from the main crown has at least two or three buds at the top. Two or three clumps of roots should be ample for most families.

The second way to obtain roots is through your nursery grower in very early spring. If a choice of rhubarb rootstocks is offered, choose the new, all-red varieties. While with some vegetables it is preferable to buy the older, more traditional varieties, with rhubarb it is better to purchase the newer varieties. 'Crimson Red' and 'Chipman's Canada Red' are particularly good, as is the standby 'MacDonald'. Both 'MacDonald' and 'Canada Red', by the way, are good for freezing. 'Honeyred', another good variety, does not send up a seedstalk, something you have to be wary of with other varieties. (Seedstalks should be cut as soon as you see them forming, as they sap energy from the roots.) The 'Cherry Red' variety is recommended for those who live on the West Coast. Incidentally, it is preferable to purchase roots rather than start them from seeds. Frequently, seeds are not true to variety.

You may want to test the pH of your soil before planting the roots, but be assured that rhubarb will do well in a range between 5.5 and 7.0. The ideal way to prepare the soil is to dig holes three feet on center, each hole being two feet deep and two feet across. Discard the subsoil. Line the bottom of each hole with six to eight inches of well-rotted cow manure, and then fill the holes with a mixture of equal parts compost and topsoil. Set the roots of this heavy feeding plant one per hole, so that the tops of the roots lie three to four inches below the surface.

If you live in northern regions, roots should be planted as soon as the soil is workable in the spring. In areas of milder climates, fall planting is practical. Since the plant is so long-lived, be sure to situate it where it will remain undisturbed for years. Every five years or so, each clump of roots should be dug up and separated. In this way you will be assured of thick, tender stalks. Plants left alone too long will lose their vitality and produce only thin stalks.

Many gardeners mulch their new and established *R. rhabarbarum* plants with decomposed cow manure in the fall. In the spring they remove the mulch, fertilize, and then replace the mulch. This is another way of encouraging thick, juicy stalks every spring.

Because rhubarb stalks, like asparagus, are the result of nutrients stored in the roots, it's important not to harvest them the first year. Harvest lightly the second year. When harvesting, always grasp the base of each stalk and pull sharply. Don't cut them with a knife. Large stubs left by cutting may become diseased and cause the rhizomes to which they are attached to rot. Beginning in the third year, harvest only for about eight weeks. Immediately after pulling the stalks off, cut the leaves from the petiole. The stalks will retain their moisture much longer.

Even though this plant is very pest-resistant, you should watch for Japanese beetle infestation. If you forget about your rhubarb plants in an out-of-the-way spot in the garden, you might one day discover the leaves have been damaged by this insect.

Crown rot might be another problem. Rot forms at the base of the leaf stalks, and wilting progresses from stalk base to stalk base until the plant dies. There is no remedy. Dig up the plant carefully to remove as many of the infected roots as possible and as much of the infected soil as possible. Burn what you are able to dig up. Be assured, though, that the possibility of crown rot is minimal.

FORCING RHUBARB

Rhubarb also permits interesting, out-of-season gardening, as it can be forced. In very early spring, simply cover the plant or plants that you want to force with drain tiles, bottomless peach baskets, barrels, or boxes. Pack 18 inches of fairly fresh manure around the boxes or baskets to generate warmth, and within a few weeks very tender, mostly blanched stalks will arise to provide you with a very early crop. If you want to start forcing earlier, place a sheet of glass atop the bottomless box or basket to provide even more heat. If you spread a straw manure around the plant, be sure to add fertilizer heavy in nitrogen;

the decomposition of hay or straw consumes significant quantities of nitrogen.

There is another forcing method specifically for those who live in a climate where winter freezes the soil. If you have an extra rhubarb plant that you plan on dividing in the spring anyway, use it for winter forcing. In November, just before the ground freezes, dig up the roots and set them in boxes or bushel baskets filled with soil and lined with plastic. Place the containers on stone or brick to prevent them from freezing to the soil and leave them outside until mid or late January. The roots should not be subjected to temperatures below zero degrees Fahrenheit, but freezing above this temperature is essential to the plant's dormancy.

Then, as you want stalks, carry each box into the cellar and let the soil thaw. At a temperature of 60 to 65 degrees Fahrenheit and with proper moisture, the stalks will begin to grow and will be ready for harvesting in about six weeks. Light is not necessary, as all the nutrients are stored in the rhizomes and fleshy roots.

Once you have harvested the stalks, keep the soil moist until the garden is workable. At that point, reset the roots in the garden. You should not harvest from those roots again that year, so they can have time to recuperate.

Rhubarb forcing is a sizable industry just outside Detroit, as well as in areas of Ohio and other states. The people in this industry say that three-year-old roots are best, although they do use older roots. Forced stalks are crisp, free from fiber, and support only insignificant leaves. And, as Cassell's *Dictionary of Cookery*, published in 1877, tells us, "Early forced rhubarb, or champagne rhubarb, as it is called, is especially prized for its beautiful colour."

Because rhubarbs add an air of tropical luxuriance to your garden, you might want to use them for decorative purposes. *Rheum rhabarbarum* and its relative *R. australe*, with 5- to 10-foot flower stalks, or the deeply lobed *R. palmatum* might be set at either side of your garden entrance or along one side of the driveway. The flower stalks, by the way, are long-lasting in flower arrangements. If Kew Gardens can use these plants decoratively, so can you. An 1888 issue of *Pall Mall* states, "In most gardens the rhubarbs are considered only in their capacity as food suppliers, but at Kew they are allowed to assume their natural character."

COOKING WITH RHUBARB

You'll find that the earliest stalks that come up in May will be the most tender. It is these that will make the best pies, tarts, and stews. Jane Doerfer, who collaborated with Marian Morash on the *Victory Garden Cookbook*, has a pie recipe that includes butter to cut down the rhubarb's acidity: Combine 2 cups rhubarb cut into 1-inch lengths (use only the pink section of stalks), 1¼ cups light brown sugar, and 1 tablespoon flour, and place in an unbaked 8-inch pie shell. Dot with 3 tablespoons butter. Cover with top crust, cut steam vents, and bake in a preheated 400-degree oven for 15 minutes. Reduce to 350 degrees and bake for 25 minutes longer or until well browned.

Then there is the June rhubarb harvest, which will coincide with strawberry picking. The result of this combination can be a tasty strawberry-rhubarb pie. Margaret Crockett, wife of the late Jim Crockett, has a recipe: Take 3 cups of firm young rhubarb stems and cut them into 1-inch pieces. Mix them with 1 cup of sugar, ¼ teaspoon of salt, ¼ teaspoon of nutmeg, 2 tablespoons of quick-cooking tapioca, and ¼ cup orange juice. These ingredients are put in a 9-inch pie pan lined with pie crust, topped with 1 cup of fresh sliced strawberries, dotted with 1 tablespoon of butter, and crisscrossed with pastry strips. The pie is baked at 425 degrees for 40 minutes and served piping hot with whipped cream topping.

Whereas rhubarb is commonly known in New England as the pie plant, it is also known as the wine plant. As early as 1788, we find a reference in Healde's *New Pharmacopoeia* to rhubarb wine. You can make a simple, wine-like drink by adding a bit of lemon and sugar to the cooked juice. It is ready within 24 hours and makes a most refreshing drink.

But there is a true wine that can be made from rhubarb. John Seymour, the well-known English advocate of self-sufficiency, considers it the finest of summer wines. Here is a recipe from *Farmhouse Fare*, a collection of recipes from the British *Farmer's Weekly*: "Wipe and cut 2 lbs. of rhubarb, put it into a large saucepan with ½ lb. of lemon balm leaves, well washed, and 4 quarts of water. Bring to a boil and boil for 30 minutes. Strain, and when lukewarm add ½ oz. of citric acid and 1 to 1½ lbs. of sugar, according to taste. Cover and let it work for 24 hours. Then carefully skim and bottle." It is ready for drinking the same day, if you wish. This makes a most refreshing and nutritious drink.

By the way, whether you make wine, stews, or pies with rhubarb, don't peel the stalks if you want to retain all of that pleasing pink coloring.

RHUUUBARB

While this sturdy plant has its many uses, so does the word itself. In slang usage, "rhubarb" has come to mean a heated argument or discussion. The word has also been used as a theatrical device by both early and contemporary play directors. A director who wants members of a crowd scene to simulate conversation often asks them to repeat one word over and over again quietly, "Rhubarb, rhubarb, rhuuubarb, rhubarrb, rhubarb."

31

LEEKS

One Sunday afternoon in mid April several years ago, I dropped in on Jon and Marianne Swan. They live in Clayton Corners, a hamlet in the southern part of the Berkshire Hills of western Massachusetts. As I walked across the lawn and toward the fences that surround their many vegetable plots, Jon hailed me and invited me into the inner sanctum of one of his patches.

He was forking carefully at eight-inch-thick layers of rotted straw and hay to uncover decidedly bedraggled gatherings of leaves that had the previous fall been dark green and shaped like quills.

"The very badge of the Welsh, this hardy leek. Have you ever tasted leek and potato soup?" he asked. I confessed ignorance of both the leek and the soup, so after he pulled the remaining straw from those biennials to expose the tops of 20 or so he'd put in almost a year ago to the day, we headed for the kitchen.

Jon rummaged around in a freezer still packed with last season's vegetables and took out a quart container of soup. Twenty minutes later he, Marianne, and I were sitting around the kitchen table eating slabs of buttered dark bread and a creamy, delicately onion-flavored soup. Time and again since then, whenever I mention leek and potato soup, people who know it invariably conjure up images of sitting before an open fire on a winter afternoon sampling the soup. A leek lover is a true enthusiast.

Allium porrum is a member of the family Liliaceae. As an allium, it's closely related to onions and garlic. This common garden leek has what appears to be a stem that is 8 to 14 inches long, pure white, and an inch or two in diameter. This stem is actually a set of edible, fleshy leaf bases that are folded closely over each other. At the base of this stem, a tuft of pure white roots grows from a bulb only slightly larger than the stem itself. The only part of this blanched plant to grow aboveground is a set of one-foot-long, dark green, flat leaves that fan out from the top of the stem to create a most attractive shape. My wife speaks of the beauty of rows of these dark green fans against a white cover of snow in her mother's garden in the Cotswolds.

The leek is traceable to ancient civilizations of the Near East. The followers of Moses bemoaned the absence of leeks from their diet as they suffered the privations of the Sinai circa 1500 B.C. The leek was probably introduced into Great Britain by the Romans, who were known to cultivate it widely. It was cultivated throughout Europe during the Middle Ages.

The leek arrived in America sometime during the eighteenth century. According to Roman's *Natural History of Florida*, the vegetable was grown at Mobile, Alabama, and by the Choctaw Indians in the region before 1775.

And as Jon said, it is the Cymric national emblem. Every March 1, Saint David's Day in Wales, all Welshmen, and, in particular, all members of the Welsh Guards Regiment, wear leeks in their hats as part of their uniform. It's worn in memory of their ancestors' victory over Saxon invaders in A.D. 540. In that battle, to distinguish their forces from those of the Saxons, the Welsh warriors wore a leek in their hats. They attributed their subsequent victory to the vegetable, and it has come down through these 14 centuries as their emblem. It might also be the source of the national colors—white and green.

Shakespeare pays homage to the leek and the Welsh in, among other plays, *Henry V*. Fluellen says to Henry in act 4, scene 7, "If your majesties is rememb'red of it, the Welshmen did good service in a garden where leeks did grow, wearing leeks in their Monmouth caps; which your majesty know to this hour is an honorable badge of the service; and I do believe your majesty takes no scorn to wear the leek upon St. Davy's Day." The King answers that he does indeed "wear it for memorable honor."

LEEKS IN AMERICA

But whereas this vegetable is not only the Welsh national emblem but also a favorite vegetable throughout Europe, in

America it remains relatively unknown and uncultivated. Most people I spoke with about leeks mentioned having seen them once in a health food shop or in a gardening book. "But grow leeks? No. I never have. Have you?"

I spoke with Howard Prussack one winter day in the kitchen of his farmhouse in Westminster West, Vermont. The snow was falling thick and heavy outside. Like many of the customers at his roadside stand, Howard was enthusiastic about leeks. He was then a young and ambitious New Yorker who had moved out of the city and married a Vermont woman, the two of them running a successful farm. Leeks represented only two percent of the Prussacks' crop, but they played their part in attracting a number of people to the roadside stand.

Because the stand was so close to Brattleboro and its relatively international community, Howard and his wife offered a range of unusual vegetables along with the standard fare, thereby attracting more people. It was only on this basis that Howard grew the leek. He considered it primarily a service to his customers.

Howard planted his first leek seeds in hotbeds in early March 1974. In late April of that year, he set out the four-inch wispy 'Conqueror' and 'American Flag' seedlings and hoped for a good crop of around 2,000 plants.

Though his customers—health-food shops in New York and Boston, as well as those who stopped at the stand—were happy enough to buy those particular varieties, he was not altogether pleased with the quality. He found that the 'Conqueror', massive as it was, did not have sufficient stem length to offer good value and that the 'American Flag' variety was too small and its leaves a somewhat unattractive green.

After five years of experimenting, Howard settled on the Harris Seed Company's 'Tivi' and 'Electra' seeds. They typically produce a 12- to 14-inch-long stem that is never less than 1 to 1½ inches in diameter. Some are even 18 inches long and 2 inches in diameter.

And they make for simple cooking and a delicate taste that is related to, though very different from, the onion. Howard pointed out that to cook them, one merely needs to slice the stem in cross sections and boil the pieces for a few moments. The cooked sections can then be served with butter or combined with soups or sauces. Many people who cannot eat onions for one reason or another find that they can eat leeks and enjoy their subtle flavor.

If they are so delicious, why don't people in America grow them more often? I asked several gardening friends. One told me that any vegetable requiring one kind of attention or another from March through September was more trouble than it was worth. Another told me he felt leeks took up too much space for too long a time. But most of the people I spoke with simply never considered growing them. The leek wasn't a vegetable with which they were familiar or for which they had a taste.

Well, I sympathize with these problems, but I find that if one has the space and time, unusual, aesthetic, and somewhat exotic vegetables that yield interesting tastes are always worth that extra bit of garden space and time. In fact, the leek doesn't require much more work than most other vegetables.

PLANTING, PAMPERING, AND HARVESTING

I have planted leeks in two ways. The English have a truly no-nonsense method. Using a crowbar or a dibber, make an eight-inch-deep hole in the ground, drop a seedling from a tray you bought at the nursery into the hole, and forget it. Rains, winds, and earthworms will see to it that the hole is gradually filled in, thus assuring that the stem will be blanched. This is a good method if you have relatively loamy soil that is mixed with a good percentage of organic matter. It worked well for me in a Connecticut garden.

But for those who enjoy pampering their vegetables there is another method. In areas of cold climates, seeds should be started in a hotbed around early March. When the seedlings are about an inch high, they should be replanted at one-inch intervals to save trouble separating the minute plants when it comes time to set them out in the garden.

Around April 1, turn the heat off in the hotbed to harden the seedlings for mid- to late-April planting. By mid April the seedlings should be about three to four inches high. They will look like blades of grass.

The ideal way to prepare the soil for leeks is to dig a trench 8 to 10 inches deep. Line the bottom with four inches of old compost, and then set the seedlings an inch or two into the compost and eight inches apart. Pull soil around these plants every three weeks or so until mid July. Each time you do this, add a small amount of 5-10-5 fertilizer (5 ounces to a 10-foot row). The pH level should not drop below 6.5; 6.7 is ideal. And have patience with the plants. They won't really take hold and grow vigorously until July.

Leeks can be harvested anytime after July, though they reach their stoutest around October. If you don't want to wait so long for fresh leeks in the second and subsequent years, leave what smaller plants you haven't harvested in the soil through the winter. In areas of severe winters, cover them with sufficient straw, and a good percentage will survive and make good eating that spring and early summer before they begin to bolt. With careful planning, you can have leeks during much of the growing season. For those who live in regions with mild winters, seeds should be sown in the autumn for spring and summer harvest.

This hardy vegetable is relatively free from pests and diseases. The only major problem Howard Prussack had to control in the leek bed was late blight, that is, *Botrytis*. This fungus thrives in the cool, damp, late-season months of September and October. Purple dots called targets appear on the leaves. These tiny circles begin to rot and gradually expand to destroy many of the leaves and, in a few cases, the stems. Howard found spraying with bordeaux mixture to be the best control method. He had no problems with thrips and only negligible problems from onion maggots.

The main problem for the medium-size commercial grower, however, is neither fungus nor pests but the length of time the leek requires to mature. It is therefore an expensive vegetable to raise. Paul Harlow of Westminster said that it just wasn't worth it for them to tend leeks from March through September and end up selling them for no more than 35 cents each. He could take the same plot of ground and get two or three crops of lettuce, each head of which would bring in 50 cents.

But for the home gardener, this need for efficiency isn't quite as pressing. If you have the space, the leek is a hardy, attractive vegetable that remains largely free from disease and pests throughout the growing season. It provides a most unusual and delicate flavor at table and stores well in the freezer.

But whether you eat leeks in leek and potato soup or cock-a-leekie, simply boil the stems as you would asparagus, or eat them cold as in leeks vinaigrette, you are joining a long and illustrious line of leek lovers. Picasso, obsessed with hunger during the Occupation, lovingly painted representations of leeks. But 2,000 years before him, Aristotle praised the leek and Dioscorides, the physician, recommended it to improve the voice. Nero enthusiastically embraced this advice. Pliny reports that in preparation for song or oratory, Nero would abstain from all food but leeks and oil for several days a month. And given the cost of health care today, we would do well to heed this seventeenth-century English proverb (by the way, Lide is March, and ramsons are wild garlics):

Eate leeks in Lide,
And ramsons in May,
And all the yeare after,
Physitians may play.

32

CHILDREN IN
THE GARDEN

They race through the soil I just rototilled and planted, they bulldoze the lettuce with their Tonka toys, they come into the house beaming with pride to present us with 108 green tomatoes they just picked. Children *in* the garden? Tell me how to keep them out.

While our son Nate has done his share of picking the wrong tomatoes, plowing under the freshly planted seedlings, and walking on the rows, we've managed to introduce him to the wonder of growing things. We're convinced that with careful planning, good gardening techniques, and lots of encouragement, anyone can experience the pleasures of gardening with children.

The first thing you can do with your child is to ask him if he would like to have his own garden. If he responds with enthusiasm, involve him in the selection of vegetable and flower seeds as well as tools. Grandparents who live at a distance, but who would like to encourage their grandchildren, could send seeds from their area. Or, during a spring visit, they could provide potted plants or starter packs with seedlings already established.

When selecting vegetable seeds with and for your child or grandchild, keep three things in mind: What vegetables does he enjoy eating? What plants mature relatively quickly? Which plants can be cared for easily? Our son, for example, enjoys picking edible-podded peas, carrots, lettuce, beans, cucumbers, and sometimes a tiny zucchini. These vegetables also reach maturity quickly and have few pests or diseases.

If your child would like flowers as well as vegetables in his garden, nasturtiums are a particularly good choice. They grow quickly from seed sown directly into the soil and rapidly develop into luxuriant mounds of flowers and foliage. The flower is also edible, a fact that often intrigues a child. Sunflowers are also wonderful. Although they take the full growing season to mature, they are so dramatic in size that children enjoy watching them grow higher and higher. You might also consider calendula, white alyssum, cosmos, nicotiana, or morning-glories.

Many plants can be grown satisfactorily from seed, but others should be purchased as established plants. Children enjoy cherry tomatoes, for instance, but, if started from seeds indoors six to eight weeks before planting out in the garden, a child may lose interest and stop caring for the seedlings. During the first year or two of your child's gardening experience, it's especially important to do everything possible to help him succeed.

If you live in the city and can only garden in pots on the balcony, introduce your child to plants that have been specially hybridized for their small, compact growth habits. If you would like to plant cherry tomatoes, consider Harris's 'Presto' or Burpee's 'Tiny Tim' or 'Basket King'. Cucumbers, particularly the new bush types that do not send out lengthy vines, are also good for balcony gardens. You could also encourage your child to grow herbs or nasturtiums in pots. If your balcony is shady, impatiens is a good shade-loving plant.

The greater the variety, the better. One never knows what will attract a child's interest. One year it was Nate's bean house; the next year it was one single petunia plant. He and his schoolmates visited a nursery where the nurseryman gave each of them a single petunia plant. We set our son's plant into one of our perennial borders, and not a day went by that Nate didn't check his plant. When I watered the rudbeckia and coreopsis, he watered his petunia. When I deadheaded the lavender or marigolds, he took the seed pods off his petunia. It was a theme for the entire summer.

If you are a neighbor with no children, give the child next-door a plant, and you may have a friend for life. The things you could teach that child are almost limitless—responsibility, pride, a respect for life, an awareness that plants are living, changing, and beautiful things with special needs and preferences.

DESIGNING A CHILD'S GARDEN

Once you have decided what seeds and plants to buy, you can begin to lay out the design of your child's garden with him. If at all possible, open up a new garden area that is close to, but separate from, your garden. If that's not possible, mark off a section of your vegetable garden with stepping stones, an informal fence or a marigold border. A child needs to know just what space is his.

You don't have to be rigid about the shape of the garden. Friends of ours have three daughters, and when their girls were all under 10 years of age, they prepared three 4-by-12-foot gardens that were separated by strips of lawn. Each garden had an arched or semicircular end that approximated the shape of a stained-glass window. The gardens were planted with flowers and vegetables in blocks rather than rows, so they indeed resembled stained-glass windows when surveyed from the limb of a nearby apple tree.

Be inventive in your design, and encourage your child to come up with ideas, too. Try curvilinear shapes, or a circle 10 feet in diameter that could have a small herb garden in the center. (You can outline the shape with your garden hose.) Consider including a fence somewhere in the design that can be used to support trailing plants like cucumbers or morning-glories.

CHILDREN'S TOOLS

Once you have chosen specific seeds and have plants and a design in mind, your child will need some tools. (Here is another way grandparents can help in encouraging their grandchildren to garden.) The Smith and Hawken catalog is an excellent source for children's gardening tools. According to their catalog, "One of the frustrations for children in beginning gardening is that no one has taken seriously the making of children's tools. Tools are either cheap or inadequate, or children are left to use adult's tools which are large and ungainly."

The catalog goes on to say that "down-scale tools give the child an immediate sense of purpose and effect of normal tools. . . . The T-handles permit small hands a good two-handed grip. Their durability allows years of use and wear."

Whether you buy a fine spade, fork, or iron rake from Smith and Hawken, or an onion hoe, a hand trowel, or "ladies' gardening tools" from the local hardware store, take the tools you give your child seriously. If you think he'll need a cart, for example, get a two-wheeled bucket type rather than a wheelbarrow; it will be easier for him to manage alone. Look carefully at the tool with respect to your child's strength and size. He'll need good implements to work with, just as you do. Give your child the best tools now, show him how to use and maintain them properly, and his gardening experience will be much enhanced. And years later he'll have a set of tools to give his own children, or maybe he'll give them back to you when you are older.

Your child's tools will also be useful to grandparents or anyone in the family who, because of a handicap, cannot use adult-scale tools. If you garden on a balcony or patio, you'll also find these tools useful.

PLANTING AND HARVESTING

When the soil is dry enough in the spring to be tilled, prepare it for planting with your child. After the soil is turned, show him how to enrich it so that his plants will grow well. Add generous amounts of decomposed compost or cow manure. This is an important step, because nothing will discourage a child more than putting a lot of time and effort into a garden, only to end up with poor results.

When it comes time to plant, show your child how to mark out the rows or planting blocks and how deep and far apart each variety of seed or plant should be set. But let *him* do the planting. With his nimble little fingers and the very real patience a child has when truly involved, he can do a good job of planting. Consider planting in blocks rather than in rows. Such dense planting, where the leaves of individual plants touch each other, creates shade sufficient to discourage many weeds.

You might also try planting seeds so that plants come up in

interesting new ways. For example, one summer Nate and I made a bean house that even Jack would have admired. We set five beanpoles into the soil perpendicularly, in the shape of a semicircle. The open side faced north; the back faced south. The distance between the two outermost poles was about eight feet. Once the poles were in place, I tied another long pole across the tops of the two outermost poles, and then tied baling twine from that crosspiece to the top of each pole, thus forming a latticework roof. We then planted six 'Kentucky Wonder' pole beans at the base of each pole.

Weeks later the bean vines had climbed to the top of each pole and onto the latticework at the top, and they were in full bloom. His house was complete. On more than one hot summer day, he sat in the shade of his bean house on a stump of wood I had placed there for a seat. There he could pluck and eat beans to his heart's content.

To help your child distinguish young weeds from young vegetable seedlings, you might have him plant a few seeds in carefully labeled flats a few days before he plants seeds in the garden. That way, when seeds come up in the garden, he'll be able to look at the labeled seedlings in the flats and know what he's looking for in the garden.

Transplanting from flats also has its tricks. When transplanting tomatoes, petunias, marigolds, or even cucumber seedlings, mulch the young plants after setting them in the ground. Use two to three inches of pine needles to retain moisture and, at the same time, allow for aeration of the soil's surface. Leaves or lawn clippings will prevent aeration and also attract slugs. If you are concerned about making your soil too acidic with pine needles, rake them up from the garden after the plants are established.

If your child plants in blocks rather than rows, and uses mulch throughout the growing season, there will be fewer weeds for him to eradicate. Like adults, a child will become discouraged if weeds persist and eventually overrun the garden. Don't expect your child, in this first gardening experience, to take sole responsibility for keeping weeds out. Help him, but don't take full responsibility yourself, either.

Too many people plant their gardens in early spring and then fail to take advantage of planting times later in the season.

July and early August are still good times to sow seeds of bolt-resistant lettuce, carrots, and cucumbers as well as a second planting of peas and radishes—any vegetable, in fact, that will mature before the early-autumn frosts in your area. (See chapter 26.) Take up the old pea vines and put in the new lettuce.

My own inclination regarding chemicals and commercial fertilizers (other than those that are wholly organic) is to stay away from them completely. Use compost or decomposed cow manure to build the soil or to side-dress established plants. To control insects, show your child what beetles and bugs to look for and how he can kill them by hand. This approach can work in a small garden.

There is an interesting project your child might want to use for insect control. Some companies sell praying mantis egg sacs through the mail. If you order them in late winter, they will arrive in time for incubation. The maturing creatures can then be set loose at the appropriate time in your child's garden. While the praying mantis may not entirely rid the garden of insects, it will certainly help, and it will also add another interesting facet to your child's gardening knowledge.

Once the peas and beans and carrots are ready for harvesting, show your child how to gather the vegetables, and then show him how to cook them. Together, we harvested, blanched, and then froze many of Nate's beans. On more than one wintry evening we sat down to a meal, part of which was made up of his beans. He got more than a little pleasure out of that fact, and, of course, so did we.

You may not keep your child's Tonka toys out of your spinach, and he may still run amuck in that soft, newly turned earth, but with his own garden, you are helping him make a step in the right direction—toward respecting nature, the soil, and the plants that give us food. Show your child the joys of gardening, and you have given him a gift for life.

INDEX

ABOUT THE AUTHOR
AND ILLUSTRATOR

GORDON HAYWARD had an early introduction to gardening as a child helping in his family's orchard in Connecticut. He has been designing landscapes and writing about gardening since 1979. In 1984 he gave up a 17-year career as a teacher of writing to start his own landscape business in southern Vermont. Since then he has created and restored many gardens throughout New England. He also spent a year restoring a garden in England, and has led three garden tours to Great Britain. Hayward's articles on gardening and other nature subjects have appeared in *Harrowsmith, Horticulture, American Horticulturist, Fine Gardening, Country Journal,* and *Cape Cod Life* magazines. His own garden surrounds a 200-year-old farmhouse in Westminster West, Vermont, where he lives with his wife Mary and son Nate.

GORDON MORRISON is widely recognized as one of the most accomplished natural history artists in the U.S. He has illustrated more than a dozen books, including *Newcomb's Wildflower Guide, The Birdwatcher's Companion, A Guide to Eastern Forests,* and *The Curious Naturalist.* His work has appeared in numerous magazines, including *Horticulture, Ranger Rick, Organic Gardening, New York Conservationist, Country Journal,* and *Yankee.* He has created murals and dioramas for public and private educational facilities, and his fine art work appears in galleries and collections throughout New England and the East Coast. He lives with his wife Nancy and their three children in North Attleboro, Massachusetts, where he keeps his home studio.

WHETSTONE PUBLISHING is an independent book publishing company located in Brattleboro, Vermont. Its other books include *Ask Anne & Nan*, a book of household hints from Vermont, and *Wines of New England*, a travel guide and tasting diary. Whetstone's sister imprint is Vitesse Press, the nation's leading publisher of books about bicycle racing.